A FOOT IN THE DOOR

KATHARINE HANSEN, PhD

A FOOT
IN THE
REVISED
DOOR

[NETWORKING YOUR WAY INTO THE HIDDEN JOB MARKET]

TEN SPEED PRESS
Berkeley | Toronto

This book is dedicated to Theodore Stewart Fries Jr., a very special young man whom I am proud to claim as a member of my personal network.

I would like to thank Dr. Rebecca Oliphant for suggesting informational interviews as an assignment for my class.

I thank the many members of the National Association of Colleges and Employers (NACE) and members of NACE's Jobplace online discussion group as well as members of the Career Management Alliance for sharing their survey responses, stories, comments, and wisdom. Thanks also to Michael Kaplan and Jennifer Sumner.

As always, I thank my students at Stetson University who inspire my writing. I especially thank those who shared their informational interviewing experiences.

And thanks and love always, of course, to RSH.

For up-to-date information about networking, please visit www.quintcareers.com.

Copyright © 2000, 2008 by Katharine Hansen

Ten Speed Press
PO Box 7123
Berkeley, California 94707
www.tenspeed.com

Distributed in Australia by Simon and Schuster Australia, in Canada by Ten Speed Press Canada, in New Zealand by Southern Publishers Group, in South Africa by Real Books, and in the United Kingdom and Europe by Publishers Group UK.

Cover and text design by Tracy White
Typesetting by Tasha Hall

Library of Congress Cataloging-in-Publication Data
Hansen, Katharine.
    A foot in the door : networking your way into the hidden job market / Katharine Hansen.—Rev.
        p. cm.
    Summary: "A guide to networking geared toward recent graduates and young career changers"—Provided by publisher.
    Includes index.
    ISBN 978-1-58008-892-3
    1. Job hunting. 2. Social networks. 3. Career development. I. Title.
HF5382.7.H354 2008
650.14—dc22
                        2007051012

Printed in the United States of America
First printing this edition, 2008

1 2 3 4 5 6 7 8 9 10 — 12 11 10 09 08

CONTENTS

INTRODUCTION

As I have considered what has changed about networking since the first edition of *A Foot in the Door* was published in 2000, my starkest realization is that networking has become even more important to getting a job than it was when I first wrote the book. Perhaps as a coping mechanism in the face of a constantly changing technological and global economy, the importance of building relationships has come to the fore in every area from marketing to politics. Job hunting is no different. In fact, while technology seems to make people yearn for face-to-face interactions, it is also the driving force behind the most significant trend in networking since the first edition of this book—online networking, using various tech-based tools, venues, and online communities. This new interactive networking setting—largely characterized by the term Web 2.0—is the subject of three additional chapters in this new edition. One chapter covers personal branding and building networking visibility; the second tells how you can enhance your networking by increasing your chances of being found in an Internet search; the third describes the world of online social/business communities and networking.

I did my first real networking in the early 1980s in the form of informational interviewing. I had learned about the concept from Richard Nelson Bolles's *What Color Is Your Parachute?*, which was already a classic in the career field and has since gone on to even greater success and recognition. It was when, as a college instructor, I began to teach my business communication students about networking and assigned them to conduct informational interviews that I truly began to see the power of networking.

My initial inspiration for the first edition of *A Foot in the Door* sprang from my excitement when I observed my students putting in practice what I had taught them about networking. They were blown away by their success with networking and informational interviewing. They used these tools to affirm career choices, avoid inappropriate options, try on careers, gain valuable insider information—and, most important, make contacts. Most students attained a solid network of contacts and insider information that enabled them by graduation time to approach employers with a clear advantage over other job seekers. Having reinstated the assignment after a five-year hiatus from teaching, I found that in the new millennium I could still expect several students every semester to receive internship and job offers as a direct result of their networking and informational interviews. In short, networking can be a life-changing activity. It is my hope that this book will guide readers through this invaluable process.

My partner, Randall Hansen, and I have demonstrated our commitment to tools of job seeking through the books we've authored and especially through our website, Quintessential Careers, one of the oldest and most comprehensive career development sites on the Web (www.quintcareers.com). The first edition of *A Foot in the Door* was the impetus to significantly build the networking resources of Quint Careers. In turn, Quint Careers has become a bubbling cauldron of much of the new information I've added to this updated edition.

This new edition is designed to give you lots of ideas about where and with whom to network. For the revision, I surveyed 240 individuals—122 career professionals and 118 job seekers—to learn about their networking experiences and ideas—and they contributed generously and abundantly. *A Foot in the Door* guides you through the process and over the obstacles of networking. The informational interviewing section is arguably the most comprehensive resource available on how to conduct an informational interview. The book provides numerous networking tips you may not have thought of and testimonials from successful networkers. It touches on the special needs of underrepresented groups and the importance of follow-up in the networking process.

Please consider me a member of your personal network. People in your network should provide you with advice and support. I offer you both in *A Foot in the Door*. I wish you much success as you build your network.

—Katharine Hansen, PhD

PART ONE

NETWORKING:

WHAT, WHY, HOW, WHO, WHERE, AND WHEN

CHAPTER 1

WHAT IS NETWORKING?

It's All about Relationship Building

Networking is a lot like sales and marketing, and all three are about establishing and cultivating personal relationships. Maybe you're uncomfortable with the idea of marketing and selling yourself. But you're probably a lot more comfortable with the idea of making friends and talking to people. That's what networking comes down to: talking to people, making friends, building relationships—all with a little self-promotion and sales savvy thrown in. "Before it was called networking, it was just being friendly and interested in people," observes Nelson Barnett, director of the Lyon College Career Development Center. When one of your contacts has some promising career information to impart, the first person he will want to tell is a friend—you, if you've successfully built the relationship.

Networking doesn't mean asking everyone you run into if she knows where the job openings are. It means establishing relationships for mutual support and sharing ideas, advice, and referrals to those with hiring power.

Leslie Smith of the National Association of Female Executives defines networking as the process of "planning and making contacts and sharing information for professional and personal gain." The key word is "sharing." Many individuals are uncomfortable with the notion of networking because it feels like "using" people. Successful networking doesn't mean milking your contacts for all they're worth; it means participating in a give-and-take. Networking is at its most effective when both the networker and the contact benefit from the relationship. Even if your contacts do not benefit immediately from knowing you, they should gain something from the relationship eventually.

We've all heard the old expression: "It's not what you know; it's who you know." The suggestion is that no matter how smart and talented you are, you don't have the same competitive edge in the job market as someone who is well connected with the people who possess hiring power. There is some truth in that adage. Networking is the process through which you get connected and build relationships with people who can help advance your career. Not everyone you encounter in the networking process has hiring power; in fact, most members of your network probably will not have hiring power. These intermediaries give you valuable information and career advice while steering you toward opportunities and the honchos who do hire. They make it possible for you to connect with those with hiring power for this reason: you are always more likely to be considered by a hiring manager if you are referred by a mutual acquaintance than if you tried to approach the hiring manager "cold."

Do you already have to know a lot of people to be able to network effectively? Absolutely not. All you have to do is want to know more people than you already do, people who can assist you in your quest for your ideal job. You should also be willing to do as much as you can to encourage others to want to get to know you and help you. It takes only one person to start your network, because that person can refer you to others. If each new person you contact does the same, your network will expand exponentially.

Some of the most successful people network. A consummate politician, former President Bill Clinton is said to have maintained an index-card system containing the names of everyone he had met since college. For folks like Clinton, networking is more than a job-hunting technique trotted out when needed; it's a way of life. The most successful networkers make it a lifestyle, but you can benefit from networking even if you don't do it all the time.

Networking is viewed as even more important than such hallowed job-hunting tools as resumes. Professional resume writer Susan Britton Whitcomb, author of *Resume Magic* (Jist, 2006), suggests that a resume is not at its most effective when it precedes your interview with a hiring manager. "A better strategy," Whitcomb writes, "is to establish rapport with the hiring manager before submitting a resume. For most people, an initial face-to-face or voice contact is more engaging than print-on-paper."

Your goal should be to form relationships that are so powerful that your contacts feel invested in your success—and you in theirs. On his CareerLab website (www.careerlab.com), William S. Frank recalls a successful job hunter he once met who said, "I create relationships. The relationships create jobs."

College career counselor Tracy Hakala tells a story of how building and maintaining relationships paid off for a candidate her office hired:

> A [career services] colleague at another university was interested in seeing other career services offices while she was visiting family on holiday. She was very professional in contacting [our office], making arrangements, and visiting us. At this point we had no position openings, nor did this person indicate that she was looking for different employment. She later made it a point to talk to our director at a professional association conference. Plus she kept in contact with me through email. When she saw that we had a position opening a few months later, she indicated her interest, applied, and was eventually offered the position. It really did make a difference when her application came around. We already knew a little about her and had been impressed with her professionalism. I think it gave her an edge over the other candidates.

Finding a job is far from the only reason for networking; as placement counselor Judy Robinson points out, "Networking not only assists you in finding available positions in the field, but it also provides you with the opportunity to learn more about the profession and gain insights into trends in the industry that can be helpful in the interviewing process." Career specialist Robin Hammond comments, "I find that my greatest professional growth recently has occurred as the result of networking and not as a result of my professional work."

Before moving further in our discussion, it will be useful to look at the types of networking and how they fit into the overall process. At its most basic level, networking can be divided into two categories:

- **Developmental networking:** Networking for further contacts and referrals

- **Strategic networking:** Direct networking that lays the foundation for hiring

Considerable overlap can occur between these categories, but if you want to determine the best way to make contact, it pays to have a sense of the kind of networking you're doing.

Let's look at some scenarios and how they fit these categories.

Leslie, a college junior, was concerned about getting a job upon graduation. She initiated developmental networking by speaking with her immediate family and friends to ask them for ideas about employers she might approach and other people she might contact. Her networking paid off, resulting in dozens of suggestions. She then

==========={FOOT NOTE}===========

As you prepare to network for the first time, pump up your self-esteem as much as possible. Later in this book I will discuss confidence building in more detail. Confidence will help make you a successful networker, and a healthy ego can provide a suit of armor to shield you from the occasional rebuffs you will inevitably encounter.

embarked on strategic networking by contacting some of the employers and setting up informational interviews, which proved highly effective (see part 4). Some of the referrals she received were not people with hiring power but were contacts whom Leslie could add to her network. She phoned, wrote to, or emailed many of the people who had been referred to her, and as a result she obtained more ideas, more names, and more suggestions of employers with whom to conduct informational interviews. Thus, she repeated the cycle that started with developmental networking and led to strategic networking.

John decided he was burned out on his job as a systems analyst and felt he was ready for a change. He wanted to make a major career shift, but he did not know many people in the field he was considering. For him, developmental networking started with joining a professional association for his new field and attending a social event specifically geared toward networking. He made the rounds at the event, introducing himself to many members and exchanging business cards with them. Armed with many new contacts, he began to phone his new acquaintances for lengthier conversations. Some of the phone conversations were just that—chats on the phone—but John's contacts usually gave him useful information and additional referrals. Other people John called suggested that they meet for lunch or that John come to see them in their offices. Those strategic networking meetings, too, resulted in more referrals and solid leads.

Katrina liked her job but felt she was stagnating and not advancing. She wanted to stay in her field but felt career progress might be faster with a different company. Unfortunately, her job kept her too busy to attend events where she might network. She was also somewhat shy and not totally comfortable with the idea of networking. Katrina was, however, a member of several Internet online discussion groups, which served as her venue for developmental networking. She also joined a networking group on the Internet that gave her names of others in her field. Through her "virtual" conversations with her online colleagues, Katrina learned of several job possibilities, got the *names of a number of contacts, and obtained some valuable advice that propelled her toward strategic networking and learning how to break in at one of her dream companies.*

If we were to outline the process that Leslie, John, and Katrina each followed, the plan might look like this:

DEVELOPMENTAL NETWORKING

- Begin constructing your network by compiling a list of possible contacts.

- Strategize how you will connect with these people—in person or by letter, email, or phone. See chapter 3.

- Expand your network and prepare for strategic networking by asking contacts for advice and especially referrals. Ask your contacts about the best way to approach the referrals they've given you. Even more valuable is the network contact who is willing to pave the way for you with referrals by contacting them and introducing the idea that you would like to connect with them. It's this kind of introduction that Debra Feldman of the JobWhiz, an executive talent agent and executive job search expert, does with her clients: She initiates a connection for a client by setting up a telephone introduction to a targeted networking contact, then follows up with an email selling the contact on meeting with Feldman's client. Finally, Feldman sets up the meeting between her client and the contact. It's a highly effective practice, as middle-school teacher Laura Landes of Louisville, Kentucky, notes, "I have been amazed at how doors open when someone I know puts in a good word for me."

- Follow up your initial contacts with thanks and progress reports.

- Arrange meetings and informational interviews with second-tier contacts your network has referred you to. These new contacts will likely be in a better position than your initial contacts to propel you toward being hired.

- Solicit additional referrals from your second-tier contacts.

- Maintain contact with all promising members of your network, continually updating and thanking them, while seeking new advice and referrals.

- Once you've landed that job, tell your contacts the good news. Continue to maintain relationships with your preemployment network while adding new contacts from your new workplace.

CHAPTER 2

WHY IS NETWORKING SO IMPORTANT?

The Hidden Job Market: The 75 to 95 Percent of Jobs That Are Never Advertised

What's the average person's image of the traditional job-hunting process? Perhaps responding to want ads and Internet job listings and posting lots of resumes online or sending them out cold to likely employers? Most of us know enough about how the job market has changed to realize that such an image is rather antiquated. We know that the job seeker who answers ads, makes cold contacts with employers, and then sits back to wait for results will probably have a long wait indeed. Networking has been touted as a vital part of the mix for more than two decades now. ExecuNet reported that a survey of professionals revealed the top source for job interviews to be networking contacts (46 percent of respondents), followed by Internet job listings, and distantly trailed by unsolicited contact from a recruiter. A separate survey of 181 search firms provides additional insight into the value of a strong network. According to this survey, 63 percent of all executive job openings were filled with a candidate who was sourced through networking during the prior twelve months. Surveys in the years since networking has gained a foothold consistently report that at least half of all jobs come from networking.

Other research asserts that networking ability affects the length and ease of the job search. But how many of us know why networking is so important and why the traditional methods are no longer enough?

It's because the vast majority of job vacancies—estimates range from 75 to 95 percent—are hidden from the average job seeker. These positions are never advertised and are part of the "hidden" or "closed" job market. You can find out about these jobs only through word of mouth, and word of mouth means networking. The kinds of jobs that are advertised are probably not the ones you want. They tend to be the most competitive, yet lowest-level and poorest-paying positions. The better jobs are rarely advertised; they are most likely ferreted out through networking.

Why Most Employers *Don't* Advertise

Employers' reluctance to advertise is partly tied to the economy. Despite fluctuations, unemployment numbers remain relatively low in the United States. With the vast majority of the adult population employed, employers assume not many prospective workers will be scanning the want ads and Internet job postings. With a limited audience for their ads, employers are disinclined to spend money on advertising for workers.

The second reason is more psychological. The people who read want ads are looking for jobs. While it might seem that an employer offering jobs and people looking for jobs are a perfect match, that's not often the case in the employer's mind. The employer has to wonder, Why is this person looking for a job? The answer that pops into the employer's head, whether fairly or not, is probably not a positive one. People look for jobs, many employers believe, because they are unhappy losers, job-hoppers, or unproductive malcontents who blame poor performance on their employers and believe switching jobs will solve their problems. Employers would rather go after people who aren't necessarily looking for work. In the employer's mind, those people will be successful, productive contributors to the company's bottom line.

Employers also know that the best candidates are likely to be those referred to them through word of mouth. An average company gets 50 percent of its new hires from a pool of internal candidates and referrals, Taleo Research reports. It is only when employers are truly desperate to fill an opening that they place an ad.

"The last place I want to pull applicants from is the classified ads of major newspapers," observes Ohio State University career counselor B. J. O'Bruba. "Classified ad applicants are unreferred, untested, and unknown. The first place I look for applicants is within my current or previous organizations or among applicants who were referred to me by professional colleagues and acquaintances. These applicants are better referenced, tested, and known." Peggy Killian, director of Career Services at Elmhurst College, agrees," I have discovered through experience that I will hire only people I know through networking."

Career expert Howard Figler similarly notes, "I would always rather have a recommendation from a friend or colleague because it is easier to believe what that person is telling me. Compared to wading through inflated, distorted, dressed-up resumes from people I know nothing about, a referral from someone I know is pure gold."

Further, busy employers simply don't have the time to wade through the mountains of resumes an ad is likely to produce, especially an Internet ad, which can draw thousands of responses because of the relative ease of responding to such an ad. Employers often find it far more efficient to ask their employees and other members of their personal networks to refer high-quality candidates to them.

Finally, the process of defining job vacancies can take a long time. In some companies, a year or more can elapse between initial conceptualization of a job and actually filling the position. Thus, at any given time, theoretical positions may exist within an organization, but the formal mechanisms of funding, structuring, and writing a job description for the position mean that the job cannot yet be advertised. That's another reason networking is so valuable. If you can tap into a job in its embryonic stages, you will have a huge advantage over those who wait to answer ads. Let's say Megabucks Corporation is planning a position that you're well qualified for, but the firm is six months away from advertising the job. You don't know about the position, but your networking efforts lead you to a key person, Joe Honcho, at Megabucks. After talking with you, Honcho attends a meeting and tells his colleagues, "Hey, I just met someone who would be great for that position we're working on." The management team may even decide to reshape the job to fit your unique qualifications. With his team's blessing, Honcho gets you in for a series of interviews. Megabucks still may not be able to hire you until all the t's are crossed and the i's dotted, but once the job is official, you are in—all before Megabucks even had the chance to advertise the position. Laura Hashim, employment counselor with the New York State Department of Labor, relates a real-life example of getting into the pipeline before a job was advertised: "I called a college friend I hadn't seen in a year just to see how she was, and she asked me to send my resume to her boss. Her boss was about to advertise a position being vacated the next month. I was the only person interviewed and got the job."

{FOOT NOTE}

"Networking is the way to go for not-so-obvious occupations," observes engineering placement recruiter DeLynn Davenport. "I am a recruiter, but I am looking for a position that will make use of my French degree (and isn't teaching or translating). I have gotten quite a few leads from my coworkers and people who work for international companies and government agencies."

CHAPTER 3

HOW TO MAKE CONTACT

Part 2 details how to network once you've made contact, but here we examine ways to make initial contact. In the survey I conducted for this book, 74 percent of career professionals and 80 percent of job seekers found in-person networking to be most effective. However, it's often necessary to initiate a networking contact in another way—through phone, email, or letters—before landing an in-person meeting. As soon as you add new people to your network, ask them what type of communication they prefer for future contacts.

In Person

In-person networking generally occurs at two different stages of the networking process. You may talk with folks face-to-face when you are initially seeking referrals and ideas, as Leslie from chapter 1 did with her circle of friends and John did at the networking event he attended. The second stage occurs when those contacts lead to face-to-face meetings (lunches, informational interviews) with the people you're referred to, usually after an interim step in which you call, write, or email these referrals. Numerous venues for making in-person contact are suggested throughout this book, especially in chapter 5.

Mail

A well-written letter can be the best route when you are contacting someone you've been referred to but don't know at all or when you contact someone cold. It's a fine way to introduce yourself and state in an eloquent way your reason for contacting the recipient. Many people are more comfortable with a letter because it is less intrusive than cold calling, and you don't have to worry about playing telephone tag or about getting past a gatekeeping secretary, receptionist, or assistant. Bear in mind that if you write a letter (a sample appears in chapter 12), you will still have to follow up with a phone call. You never want to place the burden of contacting you on the person you've written to. While it's perfectly possible that the recipient will pick up the phone and call you soon after receiving your letter, you should not write your letter as though you expect that scenario to occur. Also realize that every piece of mail in a person's in-box represents a task that must be handled (even if the task is simply tossing the letter in the trash). Make your letter as concise and to-the-point as possible.

Personal and professional coach Richard Banfield describes his favorite technique of writing advice letters to successful people. He flatters the recipients with his admiration for their careers and accomplishments and asks advice on how to achieve the same level of success. Banfield says he invariably gets responses.

Email

With email now dominating communication in business, it is often a good choice when you are acquainted with the recipient or when you know a company's culture is especially oriented toward email, as technology companies are. People who are accustomed to communicating through email will respond well to this method. Email is also a reasonable choice because it's more immediate than a letter, yet less intrusive than a phone call; the recipient can read and respond at her own convenience. The text of the sample letter in chapter 12 is equally applicable to email messages, which are essentially letters without the business trappings. As with a letter, you should not leave the ball in the recipient's court, but, with the ease of responding to email, your recipient is more likely to respond to email than to a letter. In fact, some respondents to the survey conducted for this book indicated that contacts were more responsive to email than to other forms of communication. "People seem to be more responsive and helpful over email and the Internet, as compared to receiving phone calls," says Ford Myers, president of Career Potential, LLC. Jessica Smith, career advisor at Westwood College, Fort Worth, Texas, says she gets a good response rate by asking email contacts "for their advice or a tip they can share about their field instead of asking about open positions."

Bruce, a distance learning specialist in Oak Park, Illinois, told how email resourcefulness led to a job offer: He saw an ad for great job opportunity at a professional association in the Chicago area, but only the organization's name and post office box number appeared—no contact name or phone number. Bruce emailed his resume and cover letter to a friend at a company in which association members worked and asked her to pass them on to her coworkers so they might forward the materials to the right people at the professional association. One of the employees forwarded it to his contact at the professional association. Although the contact was located in New York, he emailed Bruce's documents to the Chicago headquarters, which arranged for an interview. "When I met with the HR director, his first questions were about how a Chicago-based job seeker contacted a Chicago-area organization via New York," Bruce related. "He stated that he was rather impressed with my networking and my diligence, and let me know that those elements played a role in getting me in for the interview." He was impressed enough, in fact, to offer Bruce a job.

Phone

If the rule is never to leave the ball in the recipient's court, it's clear that most networking roads ultimately lead to a phone call. If you loathe writing letters but are completely at ease on the phone, you may prefer the phone as your initial point of contact. Pitfalls include the inevitable phone tag of the business world and the possibility of catching your contact off guard. Persistence and politeness are keys to overcoming these obstacles.

The phone call is an essential tool in networking, so if you are uncomfortable making calls, you will most likely need to confront your fears and make yourself pick up the phone. The more you do it, the easier it will get. Practice your networking phone conversation technique on your friends. For inspiration, check out the sample phone scripts in chapter 20.

With whom, where, and when should you network? The short answer is: everyone, everywhere, and all the time. Given that such a universal approach is not always practical, the next chapters suggest ways to fine-tune your networking efforts.

CHAPTER 4

WHO SHOULD BE PART OF YOUR NETWORK?

What Kinds of Contacts Form the Most Effective Network?

It has been said that your potential network consists of all the people you already know and everyone you've yet to meet. The people who can best contribute to your network of contacts fall into several categories. These are people who can

- Give you advice, information, or referrals to additional contacts

- Tell you about specific job openings in their own companies or other organizations they may know about

- Introduce you to people with hiring power

- Hire you immediately

- Hire you sometime in the future

Try to build a network that is as diverse as possible and that includes at least a few highly influential people. Don't rule anyone out or assume that a particular individual can't help you.

If you do no other kind of networking, at least find yourself a mentor—or let one find you. A mentor is that one person who can guide you, help you, take you under her wing, and nurture your career quest. A Yoda to your Luke Skywalker. A Glinda the Good

Witch to your Dorothy Gale. What separates a mentor from the average network contact is long-term commitment and a deep-seated investment in your future. Where a typical network contact might be associated with quick introductions, exchanges of business cards, and phone calls, your relationship with a mentor is likely to involve long lunches and meetings in the mentor's office. A mentor is often in a position you'd like to be in and has the clout and connections to guide you to a similar position. She is probably someone with whom you have unusually good chemistry and who will share stories with you of her own climb to success. An effective mentor isn't afraid to criticize constructively.

To find a mentor, identify someone you admire, and test the waters by asking for advice. Be sure to reveal as much of your personality, experience, and goals as possible. Mentors are most likely to invest themselves in people who remind them a little of themselves, which is why you should never approach a prospective mentor in a state of desperation or helplessness. The mentor wants to work with someone he can respect. He may even desire to mold the protégé in his own image; this type of relationship will work as long as the mentor is not too obsessive about it and you are comfortable with the image into which you're being molded. You should have a good feel after a few meetings as to whether the rapport is right for a mentoring relationship. At that point, you can either come right out and ask the person to be your mentor, if that feels appropriate, or you can simply tell him how much you've benefited from the advice you've received so far and that you hope he will continue to share it with you. Although the mentor will tend to give a lot more than you do to the relationship, be sure to express regularly that you value and appreciate the mentor's guidance. The feeling of being needed and making a difference in a protégé's life will often be a rewarding payoff for the mentor.

Sometimes the very act of seeking a mentor can become its own networking experience, as it did for Nancy DeCrescenzo, director of a career counseling office. "An interviewer suggested I get a mentor in higher education, the field I was interested in entering," DeCrescenzo recalls. "I visited my local community college, knocked on the door of Career Services and asked the friendly guy in the office for help. He referred me to the director of career counseling at another nearby school, who in turn shared a copy of a networking newsletter that contained the posting for the position I now hold. It was a bold course of action for a frustrated job seeker that really paid off!"

For more information about finding a mentor, see the article, "The Value of a Mentor," at www.quintcareers.com/mentor_value.html.

Networking has a lot to do with looking for commonalities. Mutual interests provide openings for building relationships with people in your network. And, more often than not, members of your network share something in common with you. However, networking expert Sarah Michel suggests attending parties, functions, and meetings that are outside your usual world so you can expand your sphere of influence. Brian Uzzi and Shannon Dunlap affirm this view in the *Harvard Business Review* with research that shows that if you are building your network based on your contacts' similarity to yourself, your network may be too inbred. "Too much similarity restricts your access to discrepant information, which is crucial to both creativity and problem solving," Uzzi and Dunlap write. The authors instead recommend approaching networking from a shared activities perspective—"relatively high-stakes activities that

=======[FOOT NOTE]=======

Consultant George Moskoff advises giving serious thought to any network you attempt to construct. You will add value to your network if you consider what your contacts have in common with each other as well as with you. Think about reasons they might be motivated to help you and how you might be able to help them.

connect you with diverse others . . . including sports teams, community service ventures, interdepartmental activities, voluntary associations, not-for-profit boards, cross-functional teams, and charitable functions." Tony Abbruzzi, assistant director of the Career Services Center at the University of North Carolina at Greensboro notes that the shared activities perspective works because "boundaries [are] removed." Abbruzzi cites as an example volunteering at a Habitat for Humanity project. "You [were] in contact with people who [were] professionals and blue collar, with a college education or a high school diploma; there [were] no labels or titles. People worked and conversed while working for the good of humanity, and some very strong networking contacts [were] made." How you connect with people in these groups will vary according to your tastes and preferences. You might prefer unstructured situations that enable you to seek people out one-on-one.

In addition to identifying individuals and asking them to be part of your network, you may find that organized group membership enables you to append large networks to your own in one fell swoop (well, it might take a few swoops). Some categories of ready-made networks include

- **Groups whose members share your career or the career you aspire to.** Professional associations and organizations are the best examples of such groups, and their members are often highly effective network contacts.

- **Mixed-career groups.** Members of these groups come from all walks of life, yet a common thread has brought them together. Your local chamber of commerce or church group are examples. Even the people at your current place of employment can be part of this kind of group. In all likelihood, not everyone you work with shares your career, but the workplace can take on family-like qualities that lend themselves to employees helping each other. Mixed-career groups are beneficial because of the diversity of people and opportunities they expose you to.

- **Same-sex groups.** For both men and women, these types of groups spring up informally all the time. Maybe you go out with the guys to play golf or smoke cigars. It's not like when you were kids and had a tree house with a "no girls allowed" sign, but it's unofficially understood that the group is just for the guys. At the same time, because of women's quest for greater empowerment over the past several decades, a number of formal groups for women have sprung up, such as Business and Professional Women USA and the National Association for Female Executives. See the Resources section for an expanded list of networking groups for women.

The Very Best Kinds of Contacts for New Graduates

For the new college graduate, just about anyone associated with your college experience can form the foundation of a solid network. The cream of the crop includes

- **Your classmates.** They may seem like the competition, but no one knows you better. And since you will be going through the job search at roughly the same time, your college pals know what openings are out there. You will all encounter lots of information that you can share with each other.

- **Alumni, especially recent grads.** Recent alumni who've paved the way for you are intimately acquainted with the kinds of jobs you hope to land. Older, more established alumni may be far removed from the kind of entry-level job you'd like, but that also means they may have hiring power. One of the best ways to find alumni is to check your college's publications for updates about what alumni are doing. Look for alumni in your field and in your geographic area. Bond with them by sharing updates about their favorite professors and classes.

- **Parents.** Your parents can be rich sources of referrals for you.

- **Parents of classmates.** You knew there must have been a reason you were so polite when you visited your roommate's family back during sophomore year. Like your own parents, your friends' folks can provide a treasure trove of networking help.

- **Other relatives.** Don't be afraid to tap into the potentially rich network offered by the branches of your family tree.

- **Professors, especially your adviser.** Professors can be wonderful allies in the networking game. Teachers in your major field of study can be well connected with your career field and are certainly invested in your success.

- **Fraternity brothers, sorority sisters, and Greek organization alumni.** You've undoubtedly heard it said that you make lifelong friends in your Greek organization. That network can start working for you right away, not only with your contemporaries but also with fraternity and sorority alumni, who may be able to assist you.

- **Administrators.** They may not have been your favorite people while you were in school, but those deans and vice presidents have well-established ties with some of the most prominent people in the community and beyond. Networking efforts with administrative honchos can easily pay off.

- **Coaches.** Athletic coaches can be excellent network contacts. They care about their athletes and know lots of people.

- **Guest speakers.** The professionals who come to speak to your classes are a vast untapped resource. One of my students who was interested in a career in pharmaceutical sales approached a guest speaker from that industry after his presentation and introduced herself. She asked the pharmaceutical rep if she could send him her resume. He agreed, and she kept in touch with him throughout the last semester before she graduated. By the time she claimed her diploma, she had lined up a lucrative job with the drug firm.

- **Current and former employers.** It seems as though fewer and fewer students get through college without having a job at some point, whether during the summer or while in school. Even if the jobs you hold while in college are not in your career field, your employers can still be useful networking contacts.

- **Members of your religious community.** Whether your campus ministry or your congregation back home, your house of worship is a fine source of contacts. See chapter 5 for more.

- **Members of professional organizations.** Most colleges sponsor student chapters of professional organizations, which are rich sources of networking contacts. If your college does not have such student chapters—and even if it does—your networking efforts will benefit from a student membership in the nearest professional chapter. See also chapter 5.

- **Peer volunteers.** Volunteer work provides abundant networking opportunities at any stage of your life, and college is a wonderful time to get started, not only in making a contribution to society, but also in making some productive connections.

- **Chamber of commerce members.** If you attend meetings of the chamber of commerce in the community you wish to work in after graduation, you can make many important contacts. Consider joining the junior chamber of commerce, also known as the Jaycees, an organization especially aimed at young people. The National Junior Chamber of Commerce website (www.usjaycees.org) describes the Jaycees as "the organization of choice for men and women twenty-one to thirty-nine years of age who want the best opportunities for leadership development, volunteerism, and community service."

- **Informational interviewees.** Informational interviewing is a goldmine of networking contacts for college students. See part 4.

The Very Best Kinds of Contacts for Established Job Seekers and Job Changers

- **Members of professional organizations.** These colleagues will be among your most effective contacts. See chapter 5 for more.

- **Your past or present coworkers.** Not every workplace has the camaraderie depicted on such classic sitcoms as *The Mary Tyler Moore Show*, but most workplaces do develop family-like qualities. Your current and former coworkers likely care a lot about you and would be eager to help you make your next career move. Don't rule out people in cities where you used to work or locales in which you'd never consider working. Even if they're far away, they may know someone in the city where you do want to work.

- **Family.** Sometimes your family is networking for you without any prompting from you, as career counselor Allison Corkey discovered. "My mother called a total stranger who worked in a position that she thought that I would be good at and should aspire to," Corkey recalls. "After a thirty-

A FOOT IN THE DOOR

28

minute conversation with this person, she found out that the stranger had a part-time job coming open in a few months. My mother gave me the person's number, and I called every few days until I got an interview. I subsequently got the job."

- **Friends you're in touch with regularly.** Of course, it almost goes without saying that your friends will be important parts of your network. Don't be afraid to call upon them.

- **Old friends, such as college buddies whom you see infrequently.** You might feel uncomfortable about seeking out people you feel you've neglected for a long time, especially when you're approaching them in a state of need. Career author Donald Asher suggests holding off mentioning your networking needs when you first reconnect and then waiting ten days to ask for advice and referrals. And don't forget that they may feel just as out of touch and may be eager to reestablish your friendship. Remember that since networking is a sharing process, you may be able to give them as much as they give you.

- **Members of your religious community.** Fellowship and networking are closely related. See chapter 5.

- **Peer volunteers.** The people you meet when you're contributing to society are among the best network contacts. See chapter 5 for more.

- **Informational interviewees.** Informational interviewing is particularly helpful for those thinking of changing jobs or careers, but the process can yield results for virtually any job seeker. See part 4.

- **Neighbors.** Especially in close-knit neighborhoods where block parties and barbecues are common, neighbors can be matchless networking allies.

- **Your kids' friends' parents.** If you have kids, you undoubtedly frequently rub elbows with their friends' parents, who are fair game as part of your network.

- **Your mentor(s).** Having a mentor within your inner circle of contacts is one of the best things you can do for your career.

- **The people you "play" with.** Whether it's golf, softball, bridge, or jogging, the games people play make for ties that bind. See chapter 5 for more.

- **Community leaders and elected officials.** These pillars of the community who tend to know everyone can be quite influential.

- **Business associates, such as customers, clients, vendors, and suppliers.** The people on the fringes of your immediate employment sphere, but with whom you have regular dealings, are an often-overlooked source of networking contacts. Yet these may be the people who know the most about the comings and goings—and consequent vacancies—in your field.

- **People you admire in your field.** Though you may find it tricky to make contact with some of these folks, people you've read articles about, you've heard speak, or who have authored interesting articles themselves are wonderful additions to your network. Consider also the members of the media who cover these industry leaders.

=========================[FOOT NOTE]=========================

Many colleges and universities are establishing online communities that are tailor-made for networking. Ask your school's alumni office if it offers such a community.

- **Real estate agents, financial advisers, and others in the business-services realm.** These professionals are interested in helping you, in part because they want to keep you as a happy customer. Their business may bring them into contact with a variety of people in different fields, and they can be a useful source of contact. "Early in my career, I didn't understand the concept of using every interaction as a possible network—attorney, dentist, pastor, and so on," said Patricia Soldati, career expert and owner of PurposefulWork. com. "These sources can often take you outside your normal range of business contacts, so for that reason are invaluable in and of themselves—especially for career changers." A survey respondent offers an example: "Because I was downsized in a previous job, I was visiting with my financial planner to make a plan." Earlier that day, the financial planner was visited by someone who wanted to hire someone with the survey respondent's skill background. "I spoke with her from his office and set up an interview appointment," the lucky networker recalls. "I was offered a position after the interview."

Whether new grad or established job seeker, look for so-called "spider" or "superconnector" contacts—those people who seem to know everyone. Also seek out "bridge" contacts—those who can connect you with hiring managers.

How Many Contacts Do You Need?

The consensus among networking experts is that 250 contacts is a good goal to shoot for. Why 250? Because, supposedly, everyone knows 250 people. If you were going to, say, plan your wedding, the guest list for your side of the aisle could have 250 people on it, according to Brian Krueger in his book *The College Grad Job Hunter* (Adams, 2008). Does that mean you should feel inadequate if your network comes nowhere near that number? Of course not. Only a tiny percentage of job seekers surveyed for this book had a network that large. Of survey respondents, only 13 percent had networks of 100 people or more (and only half of those reached the magic 250 contacts).

While it's true that the more people you network with, the more likely you may be to reach your career goals, it's equally true that the quality of the relationships you build is just as important, if not more so, than the size of your network. If your core network consists of only, say, twenty-five people, but they are people well invested in you and your success, your network is probably as big as it needs to be. To start, just sit down and brainstorm a list of everyone you know who might be a helpful network contact. Open your mind to as many people as possible. Don't rule anyone out at this point. Later, you can go back if necessary and cross off people who might be too far-fetched. In my classes, I give my students three minutes to come up with as many prospective contacts as possible. Most come up with twenty-five, thirty, or more.

Your total number of networking contacts also may be less important than setting some goals, such as gaining one contact a day, three per week, or ten each month. Or set a goal to establish a certain number of contacts at each networking-oriented event you attend. That advice paid off for a student counseled by Patrick Farrell when he was director of career services at a small private college. The student was planning to attend a professional association recruitment program event. "I told her to set a goal to contact five people, if only to get their names and shake hands," Farrell relates. "Her third contact turned into a legitimate job offer. Had she not set the goal, she said she would have stood in the corner and watched all evening. But since she had set the goal, she felt compelled to get five names because she knew I would ask next time I saw her. Use whatever motivation works for you, but set a goal."

CHAPTER 5

WHERE TO NETWORK:
THE TOP 50 NETWORKING HOT SPOTS

Many events and organizations (some of which are listed in the Resources section of this book) are created specifically for networking. These organizations provide copious networking opportunities, but they tend to create only short-term contacts. Because people use these networking groups and events primarily when they are urgently seeking a job or business contacts, long-term networking relationships are unlikely to result. Thus, the best and most meaningful networking often takes place in venues that are earmarked for other purposes.

"I network everywhere I go," says corporate training and recruiting specialist Sheila Howe. "I read the paper to find social (networking) opportunities and try not to be home unless I am making phone calls, prospecting on the Internet, organizing, or writing follow-up communications. Wherever I go, I have plenty of my personal business cards with me."

Just about anywhere that people gather is fair game for networking, but here are the top thirty that successful networkers have found especially effective, followed by twenty additional promising venues:

1. **Professional organizations.** Cited as by far the most effective networking venue by those responding to the survey for this book, professional organizations provide truly superb networking settings. As career counselor John Clark points out, "Members of professional organizations are by definition in touch with their professions and tend to be aware of

upcoming openings first. Developing relationships within this framework is more than worth the effort."

"Cultivating professional relationships with colleagues in my industry has afforded me invaluable opportunities to collect new ideas and business cards and hear about career opportunities," points out Ohio State University career counselor B. J. O'Bruba. "The informal setting of conferences breeds a friendly and pro-networking environment." Echoes Vic Snyder, a career counselor at the University of Washington, "Having been in leadership positions in two different professional associations, I have consistently heard of job openings. [Professional association membership] has also helped me with social connections, since I am not overly extroverted. [Membership] gave me opportunities to be visible and to demonstrate abilities and strengths in a context that was relevant to most of the professionals in my field."

To make initial overtures toward joining an organization, career expert Don Orlando suggests contacting every group made up of members in the kind of job you'd like to have (see print and online sources for finding organizations in the Resources section). Orlando advises telling the executive director you're thinking of joining, asking what services the organization provides, thanking the director with a note, and then calling your local chapter president to ask if you can attend a meeting. Once you determine which organizations offer the best networking opportunities and support for your career, you can join your top choices.

To maximize professional associations and organizations as a networking opportunity, make yourself visible, as the networker described by Dawn Pierce, career services specialist at ITT Technical Institute, Duluth, Georgia, did: "At a professional association meeting last month, someone was attending who stood up to introduce herself and explained in her introduction that she was not yet a member and not yet in the profession, but wanted to be and then wanted to join. A lot of people, including me, spoke to her afterward to give her leads and pointers. If I had had an opening in my company, I would've been interested."

Once you've joined, be more than just a member. Volunteer to edit the organization's newsletter or coordinate the next big event. Pitch in with committee work. Offer to be program chair. Your active participation will produce indelible bonds with other members and will also allow them to see what you can do. "The best results are obtained if I become an active part of the association—take a board position, volunteer to host a committee, and so on" reports consultant Lisa LeVerrier. Vic Snyder relates that he met his current boss when he served on a professional organization committee addressing issues regarding the future of work. "I learned about her work philosophy and she mine," he recounts. "So far it is the best match I've had in a work setting."

Professional organizations often hold events specifically designed for networking, as Christine Cangiano found out. Cangiano, now director of a college career center, recalls that her first job out of college resulted from attending a professional association's networking night. "Because I did not have enough time to talk to everyone, I took down the names and numbers of the others and called them after the event," Cangiano relates. "One of the individuals thought that [my networking efforts] took so much initiative that she offered me a part-time job. I took it and a month later they hired me full-time."

Conferences put on by professional organizations also provide excellent networking opportunities, including with the superstars in your field, the conference speakers and presenters. It can't hurt to contact these folks before the conference and invite them to meet with you for coffee during their downtime.

2. **Volunteer organizations.** While there certainly are good reasons to donate your time to a good cause, the side benefit of making great contacts cannot be overlooked. Among respondents surveyed for this book, volunteer work ranked as the second most effective networking venue. Some of the best-connected professionals, in fact, place volunteer work high on their agendas, according to Dawn Baskerville, writing in *Black Enterprise* magazine. Robin Fleischer, assistant director of the Career Development Center at Transylvania University, observes, "Volunteer community activity has allowed me to network with a more diverse population within various work environments, as opposed to professional networking organizations." Volunteer work tends to be one of the more visible ways to network because it gives you an opportunity to develop and demonstrate skills—not to mention the fact that people admire your selflessness and altruism. "I have been most effective when networking in volunteer organizations," notes career consultant Cynthia Fulford. "This is where I am doing what I love, and others get to see it."

Volunteers are remembered and appreciated by people in high places whom they might not otherwise meet. Career Consultant Kathleen Natalie, of Coaching Forward in the Triad area, North Carolina, found success volunteering when she reached out to a well-connected board member: "I had been laid off and wanted to keep busy learning more about the career I planned to enter. I volunteered for a nonprofit helping with career counseling for unemployed individuals. I arranged an informational meeting with one of the board members of the organization. Because of my volunteer work, this individual arranged for me to interview with a major outplacement firm." Natalie reports that she was hired and has been in this position six years.

Volunteer work can be especially valuable for college students because of the increasing importance of obtaining experience while still in school. The experience you list on your resume does not have to be paid experience. You can learn enormous amounts and apply transferable skills through volunteer work—networking all the while. So go out there and help build a house through Habitat for Humanity. Become a literacy tutor. Produce a newsletter for a local charity. Offer your time to a community redevelopment agency. There are thousands of possibilities that will enable you to make a worthwhile contribution to society while affording you an excellent networking venue.

Watch also for volunteer events sponsored by companies you'd like to get your foot into. "I had a client who would never have made it through the online application for the company he wanted to work for, but volunteered for the company's community day of beautification," reports Elisabeth Harney Sanders-Park, president of WorkNet Solutions and co-author of *No One Is Unemployable* (Worknet, 1997), "where he served alongside company players and leaders. Through conversation, he expressed his love and respect for the company and his desire to work there. He got an interview and the job. Along the way, he had to complete an application, but by then he had become a person—not just the details—and had addressed their concerns."

3. **Charity and fundraising events.** Another way to network while contributing to charity is to attend fundraising events—luncheons, dinners, fashion shows, auctions, banquets, and balls. Although they do cost more than volunteering, these events provide yet another opportunity to add helpful contacts to your network. Writing in *Black Enterprise*, Marjorie Whigham-Desir notes that attending such events can be a huge boon to those relocating to a new area. These functions can put you on the fast track to meeting important people in a new city. Whigham-Desir advises finding out more about

the cause the event supports, as well as who the sponsoring companies are. Such research will enable you to start and maintain conversations intelligently.

4. **Civic and community groups.** Your local civic association, Lions Club, Rotary Club, Kiwanis Club, Masons, Elks, Moose Lodge, and Shriners are just a few of the community groups where networking is possible.

5. **Religious community.** Both clergy and congregation members can be part of your network. "My pastor referred me to another pastor whose church was looking for a person to start a youth group for preteen children," reports DeLynn Davenport, a recruiter for an engineering placement firm. Similarly, corporate training and recruiting specialist Sheila Howe recalls how the pastor at a new church she was joining facilitated her networking efforts. "He introduced me to the congregation and let them know my profession and job-seeking status right there in front of the congregation during a service! I was somewhat embarrassed to be

---

=[**FOOT NOTE**]=

Dan Weilbaker, a professor at Northern Illinois University, teaches "Business Golf 101," in which, the Associated Press reports, he offers such advice as

- Use the first six holes to get to know the golfers with whom you're trying to network, the next six holes to learn more about their companies, and the last six to share ideas on how you might be able to fulfill their needs.

- Don't play poorly on purpose to let your networking partners win.

- Conversely, if you really are a mediocre golfer, pick up the ball after eight shots on each hole so as not to slow down play.

---

put on the spot, but some members have reached out to assist me."

6. **Golf course.** Playing golf has been called the ultimate business relationship builder, an integral part of the business culture. Golf course behavior is often seen as a microcosm of the way business is conducted. "There's no doubt that the golf course continues to be a prime playground for the power game in business," writes journalist Anu Manchikanti in the *Minneapolis Star Tribune.* It's a way to cement your contacts in a relaxed atmosphere, away from the pressure cooker of the workplace—or even the power lunch. The game also can serve as a conversation starter off the course. Those who tout the golf course as the perfect venue for networking suggest that you will be left behind if you don't play golf. Golf can be a particularly important tool for networking within the company you already work for, especially if golf is deeply ingrained in the corporate culture. For neophytes, experts suggest lessons and practice so the game will go smoothly and not distract from networking.

7. **Tennis/squash/racquetball/basketball court.** For those who like to make connections while at play but don't favor golf, these court sports are often prime venues for networking.

8. **Health club/spa/YMCA.** There's something about the common goal of fitness that brings people together. Career counselor Diane Kohler describes an "embarrassing moment" in which she spotted an important networking contact at the gym. She had to decide "whether to hide or be seen while hot and sweaty in gym attire." Despite being mortified, Kohler came out to meet the networking opportunity head on, and it paid off—the contact eventually hired her! Try to identify the health clubs frequented by the people you most want to meet.

9. **Political campaigns.** The bonds you make with others while working to support a candidate you mutually believe in are among the strongest. Campaigns always welcome volunteers, and they offer marvelous opportunities to mingle with potential network contacts. Political fundraising events can also be mined for networking opportunities.

10. **Chamber of commerce.** Attending chamber meetings and events is one of the best ways to get to know the movers and shakers in your community. Chambers also frequently sponsor leadership classes that are superb not only for networking, but also for professional development.

11. **Your hometown.** Just click your heels together three times. . . . A research study by OI Partners showed that 80 percent of those polled found jobs in their hometowns, so, if you're living where you grew up, networking in your stomping grounds makes good sense. Look for the events that make your town your town. I grew up in Moorestown, New Jersey, where the big events were the PTA Fair and the Moorestown Horse Show. Everyone went. Those are the kinds of events at which I'd network if I still lived there.

12. **Airplanes.** "I travel the same route every week and share this experience with several other people," notes management consultant Christopher Maffett. "Once I start to recognize individuals, it makes it much easier to strike up a conversation about work and potential opportunities." Career consultant Terry Gillis cautions against overlooking airplane seatmates who might not seem like obvious network contacts. "I always seem to get seated next to little old ladies on planes and have often dismissed the idea that they could be helpful," Gillis notes. "One time, an older woman asked what I did. I told her I was a career consultant. It turned out that her son was in the business as well, and she provided

me with his name and told me to contact him. I did, and we developed a connection over time." Sitting in the boarding area waiting for a flight is also a good time to network.

13. **The favorite watering holes for your dream company/industry.** If there's a company you're just dying to work for, it makes sense to hang out where the company's denizens hang—their favorite bars, coffee shops, lunch spots, restaurants. You can soak up tons of company culture while connecting with key people who work there.

14. **Toastmasters.** This international organization serves as far more than a venue for networking. The group helps people overcome the fear of public speaking and learn skills to enhance success. It's especially good for those who are very shy about networking. Members of Toastmasters receive constructive evaluation. It's an effective way to build confidence while building your network. "I gave a speech at Toastmasters about why I would make a great employee and eventually was offered a job by someone who heard the speech," reported a career expert in Austin, Texas. Toastmaster chapters are located all over the world (check your local newspaper or phone book for one near you), but if you can't find a local branch, the Toastmasters International web page (www.toastmasters.org) tells you how to start one.

15. **Weddings.** There's nothing like a little networking when you're seated at a table full of strangers. One of those strangers could easily become a key part of your network.

==========================[FOOT NOTE]==========================

Check to see if your own company offers a Toastmasters chapter. Many organizations do so to help employees improve communications skills.

16. Cocktail parties. These gatherings aren't always the best for networking since they're primarily social events—and you do have to be wary of the booze factor—but sometimes small, festive events such as cocktail parties can present lively networking opportunities, especially when they are part of business functions. You can maximize the opportunity by learning in advance who will be on the guest list and strategizing about whom you want to get to know better. "A friend of mine mentioned in casual conversation at a cocktail party that she was job seeking," reported Jessica Litwin, career counselor at Hudson Valley Community College. "She spoke to the right person! He notified her of an immediate job opening with his legal firm, fast-tracked her resume, and, after two interviews, she landed the job. It got her out of a dead-end situation and rewarded her with a big pay raise."

17. Cruises. Some organizations offer "schmooze cruises" especially designed for networking, but even your basic vacation cruise can provide opportunities to mingle.

18. Conventions and trade shows. The business section in the newspaper for your closest metropolitan area should contain listings of these events and tell you whether they're open to the public. Look also in trade publications for your field for event listings, as well as on the website Trade Show News Network (www.tsnn.com).

=======[FOOT NOTE]=======

One of the most awkward aspects of networking at social events where food is served is trying to shake hands, exchange business cards, and talk while holding food and eating. Solution? If your main objective is to network at these events, eat before you go.

19. **Book clubs.** Spurred on by Oprah Winfrey's TV book club, community book clubs have sprung up all over the country. The stimulating intellectual atmosphere they provide lends itself well to networking.

20. **Training, continuing education, and professional development programs.** Rapid changes in the workplace mean that continuing education and even advanced degrees are desirable for many professionals; for others, further training is an absolute requirement. In the accounting field, for example, you cannot keep your certification unless you continually brush up your skills and stay on top of new tax laws and accounting practices. But even in fields where such updating is not required, lifelong learning is beneficial because it sharpens your skills and keeps you networking. You have the added advantage of networking with those who know your field the best—the people already in it. Career counselor Lori Willeford cites graduate classes as highly effective networking venues. "Not only are these individuals classmates, but they are also successful professionals and, more important, good friends," Willeford notes. "I can share my struggles, and they provide a different perspective." Faculty members and advisers are also excellent network contacts. Check with professional associations, community colleges, and universities for courses, graduate programs, workshops, seminars, and conferences that can help you refresh your skills and knowledge.

21. **College conferences.** If you're looking for prime networking situations, be sure you keep up to date with what's happening on local college campuses. Colleges and universities continually sponsor or host conferences that are superb places for networking. While some conferences are open only to members of the sponsoring organizations or college constituencies, many are open to the public. Numerous conferences include a recruiting or job-fair component. They also enable

you to expand your educational horizons and enhance your professional development. To keep abreast of conferences you might attend, watch for notices in the local newspaper, subscribe to the campus newspaper, check out the school's web page, or ask to be placed on the events-calendar mailing list.

22. **Alumni clubs, associations, reunions, events, and networks.** Whether you're a new graduate or have been out of school for a few years, it's hard to beat the networking potential of alumni clubs and associations. People's natural inclination is to do business with people with whom they have common bonds. Even small colleges have alumni chapters across the country that hold regular social events, which are wonderful for networking. If you can't find alumni groups in your area, make it a point to return to your alma mater for reunions whenever possible. To network with folks who are even more loyal than ordinary alumni in looking out for your interests, look to your fraternity or sorority. "When I move to a new city, the first thing I do is contact my national sorority's headquarters for information on the local alumnae chapter," reports Lara Cegala, coordinator of cooperative education at the University of Central Florida. "If there is not one, I then take the initiative to organize and form a new chapter. I have found that this is an effective way for me to meet new people and network with women in the community. People think sorority membership is just for collegiate women, when really alumnae benefit from membership a hundred times more. I have met some terrific women and have made many connections that have helped me personally and professionally."

23. **Ex-employer alumni clubs.** Just as college alumni clubs are valuable for networking because of the common bonds and memories you share with fellow members, ex-employer alumni clubs can offer the same benefits. A number of large

corporations have formed alumni clubs, such as the Time-Life Alumni Society and Xerox-X. Who better than people in your own current or former industry to include in your network? They know where you've been and where you could be going.

24. **Speed-networking events.** Modeled on speed dating, a speed-networking event provides participants with "a structured environment in which they can talk to people they wouldn't otherwise have come into contact with, and can quickly decide whether there is a mutual interest without the need for polite or unnecessarily long conversations," according to *Macmillan English Dictionary.* Typically, participants have no more than five minutes to talk with a prospective contact and then a whistle or buzzer signals time to move on to the next person. Ramona Collins, nonprofit and marketing professional in New York City, reports that at the end of a speed-networking evening, "I had fifteen new associates and great information on networking." Several organizations listed in the Resources section put on speed-networking events, which are also popular with college alumni groups.

25. **Organizations and events dedicated to networking.** These types of venues are increasing. To find them, check your local newspaper or try entering the name of the nearest city and the phrase "networking organization" in quotes. A search

=======================[FOOT NOTE]=======================

Don't forget that alumni magazines and other publications can be rich sources of networking contacts. You can discover long-lost classmates who might be helpful, as well as identify alumni you don't know but with whom you have something in common.

for "Orlando, Florida" "networking organization," for example, yielded a diverse collection of organizations, including
some for specific populations and people with shared interests. National networking organizations are also available
for a wide variety of interests and demographics, such as
ExecuNet for executives, Women's Professional Network for
women, Mature Workers Association for older workers, and
various groups for professionals in the same occupation and
for those of shared ethnic backgrounds. See the Resources
section for specific listings.

26. **Newspaper business section.** Almost every newspaper dedi-
cates a portion of its business section to the professional
comings and goings of people in the paper's readership area.
These sections feature blurbs, often accompanied by photos,
about people who have been hired or promoted by local companies and organizations. If you scan these sections regularly, you are bound to find someone you either know or have
something in common with. I had lost touch with a friend,
but one day I spotted her smiling face in a photo in my
local paper's business section—she had just been hired to
a new position. The news enabled me to reconnect with her.
The same process can work for anyone. If you see an item
about someone you've lost touch with, you have an excellent opportunity to call or write and say, "Congratulations on
the promotion! Let's get together for lunch soon." It's also
possible to network with strangers through these newspaper
sections, although you need a little more boldness than you
do when you contact people from your past. But let's say you
see an item about someone who went to your college and is
now working at a company you'd love to work for. It certainly
would not be unreasonable to contact the person and say,
"I'm a fellow graduate of Cornell, and I saw the item in the
paper about your new job with Zapware. Congratulations! I

wonder if you'd be interested in having lunch sometime to compare notes about Cornell and our careers."

Business sections also provide helpful networking information outside of these "comings and goings" columns. Any news of change—new markets, expansions, restructurings, retirements, mergers and acquisitions, divestitures, new initiatives, as well as new products or services, can signal that a company will have openings and that people in that company will be worthwhile targets of your networking. "Focus on anything change-related, because change means opportunity," writes William S. Frank on his CareerLab website.

27. **On the sidelines of children's sports games.** Being part of a crowd that's passionate about their children's team can be an effective networking venue, as survey respondent Jerome Janeth discovered: "After my son's game one day, a mature woman expressed how well they played. I noted her accent and realized she was from my country. We started analyzing our career needs and realized that we had compatible goals. She brings a wealth of experience, and I bring a wealth of contacts. We are now working on some wonderful career plans."

28. **While interacting with business and professional service people, such as hairstylist, barber, landlord.** It pays to tell everyone you know you are seeking a job, even service people whom you would not normally think could help you. It worked for a client of Ford Myers, president of Career Potential, LLC: "One client was desperate to break into a large pharmaceutical company's sales department, but he was having no luck. He called the place 'Fort Knox.' I urged him to ask *everyone* he knew for help and contacts. He was reluctant at first to network with anyone outside his industry. Eventually, he spoke with a wider range of people, including his barber. The

barber said, 'Oh, you want to meet so-and-so? No problem! I've been cutting his hair every Saturday for more than ten years! I'm sure I can set up a meeting for you.' Within a few days, my client was inside that pharmaceutical company, talking with the president of the sales department. All thanks to the barber." Ana M. Rios Quinn, founder and head of AIMS Coaching, Durham, North Carolina, related a similar story about a client telling a prospective landlord about her job search in response to his question about what line of business she was in. She described the type of job she was seeking. "He immediately put her in contact with someone he knew who had an opening," Quinn reported. "She went on the interview and was hired."

29. Career/job fairs. These fairs, frequently targeted at college students but sometimes at other experienced workers, comprise an interesting hybrid of traditional job-search methods and networking. Sometimes interviews conducted at these fairs or expos are planned and highly structured, but the career fair format also allows for considerable informal interviewing, where networking skills are paramount. If you attend a career fair, be prepared to answer such typical questions as "Tell me about yourself" and "Why do you want to work for _____ company or in the _____ industry?" A room filled with dozens of recruiters gives you the opportunity to build rapport and relationships with those in the most desirable companies. For more information on how to make the most of a career fair, visit Randall Hansen's web article, "The Ten Keys to Success at Job and Career Fairs," at www.quintcareers.com/job_career_fairs.html or the online chapter of Brian Krueger's *College Grad Job Hunter*, entitled "Job Fair Success," at www.collegegrad.com/job search/Job-Fair-Success/.

30. **Sports teams and leagues (softball, bowling, Ping-Pong, running, and so on).** "In a weekly running club I participate in, almost a third of the members have networked with each other to gain employment at each others' companies," said Jeff Robek, career adviser at Ohio State University.

The best of the rest:

31. **Homeowners' or tenants' associations**

32. **Travel clubs**

33. **Clubs centered around hobbies**

34. **Theme park queues**

35. **Dog shows, horse shows, cat shows**

UNUSUAL NETWORKING VENUES

Survey respondents were asked about the most unusual or creative networking venues they had employed. Here's how they answered:

- At a movie theater when the movie projector broke down
- On a ski lift
- While watching a slaughterhouse burn
- In a cadaver lab
- While getting a mammogram
- During a real-estate transaction
- In the Metro in Paris
- While serving as a dental assistant during a dental procedure
- While helping others paint a house
- At a 5K race
- During a prolonged rain delay at a baseball game
- During dance lessons
- At a scrapbooking social
- While donating blood
- In a hot tub at a conference
- At a psychic fair waiting for a tarot card reading
- Aboard a ship ("I was hosting a trade mission to Norway and had an ideal captive market because they couldn't go anywhere else!")

36. Jury duty

37. Ballroom dance lessons

38. Park benches

39. Wine tastings

40. Computer-user groups

41. Art exhibition/gallery openings

42. Waiting rooms of auto mechanics, doctors, dentists, or attorneys

43. Baptisms/christenings

44. Resorts

45. Museums

46. Your favorite beach, lake, or pool

47. Investment clubs

48. Coffee shops

49. Your kids' school functions

50. Family reunions

CHAPTER 6

WHEN TO NETWORK

For optimal career development, networking should be an ongoing process. Virtually all networking experts advise that you should not wait until you're in crisis to begin networking. When you're in serious job-hunting mode—as a new graduate seeking your first job or as a career veteran who has decided to move on—you probably won't find a scattershot approach effective. Instead, you will likely find it beneficial to set up a networking timetable to help you set goals. Two such suggested timetables follow.

Networking Timetable for New Graduates

Recommendations from college career counselors as to when college students should begin networking range from freshman year to the middle or end of the junior year. (Keep in mind that this suggested timetable deals primarily with *networking* activities related to the hidden job market; you should simultaneously pursue opportunities in the open job market, such as registering with your campus career services office, attending interviews with on-campus recruiters, and scanning want ads and job postings in publications and on the Internet.)

FRESHMAN YEAR

Certainly freshman year is not too early to get to know your professors, especially your adviser. Getting to know your peer students, a process that happens naturally in the collegiate experience, will also lay the networking groundwork in your first year of college. A good way to meet as many other students as possible is to become involved in as many organizations and activities as your academic schedule will permit you to handle. Be a curious friend; finding out as much as possible about your classmates and their interests, and about their families' and parents' occupations, can provide valuable information that you may want to recall as you get closer to graduation. Be sure to reciprocate with information that will help others. Freshman year is also the time to consider whether you might want to join a fraternity or sorority. And, if you are holding down a job to help with college expenses, establish relationships with your boss and coworkers.

SOPHOMORE YEAR

By sophomore year, you are probably beginning to narrow down your career goals, which makes this an excellent time to embark on a series of informational interviews that will help bring your career into focus. (Informational interviews are explained in depth in part 4.) You should be continuing to forge ties with professors, other students, and people you work with. You may be starting to think about obtaining an internship in your career field for the summer between your sophomore and junior years or for part of your junior year in school. That internship can yield excellent network contacts since it's presumably in your career field. If your career goal is well defined at this point, sophomore year is a good time to join a student chapter of a professional organization (or obtain a student membership to a regular chapter).

JUNIOR YEAR

Junior year is key. Start your most serious networking push now by doing the following:

- Develop your resume, if you have not done so already. You should have your resume ready so you can ask some of your network contacts to critique it. You also want to have it ready in case someone you meet asks for it. You may not be in a position to accept a job at this point, but you could gain an internship opportunity by having your resume ready. And any employer who takes your resume now, when you're not ready to accept a job, can be approached again closer to graduation. Start carrying copies of your resume wherever you go in case an opportunity presents itself.

- Begin to brainstorm a list of potential networking contacts (see chapter 4). See if you can approach that magic number of 250, but don't beat yourself up if you can't. Any number is a good start, and the list is sure to grow.

- Make a list of companies you'd like to work for, and start thinking about people you know who might be able to help you break into your dream companies.

- Find out if your campus career services office keeps a database of alumni who could be added to your network. Check the alumni files of your fraternity or sorority, too.

- Join one or more online discussion groups in your area of professional interest. Ask the members' advice on breaking into your field.

- Step up the pace of informational interviews (see part 4). You may want to set an informational interview goal; one interview a month is probably achievable while you're in school. People working in your dream companies are excellent targets for these interviews.

- Consider creating a "networking card," a business card for those not yet employed (see chapter 15), so you have something tangible to hand out to people you meet.

- Begin to introduce yourself to every guest speaker in your field of interest who visits your classes or organization meetings.

Introduce yourself to speakers in other fields who could serve as good network contacts. Give them your networking card and, if appropriate, your resume.

- Continue schmoozing with professors, fellow students, and employers.

- Become increasingly active in professional organizations.

- If you have not yet done an internship or otherwise obtained practical experience in your career field, set the wheels in motion to do so before the middle of your senior year, and establish contact with as many people as possible at your internship workplace.

- Consider establishing or enhancing your visibility, personal branding, and online presence, as well as participating in online social/business networking venues (see chapters 15 to 17). Search for and contact people in your prospective career field and preferred geographic area.

SENIOR YEAR

Networking activities should be a major focus of your senior year.

- Decide where you want to live after graduation. Most soon-to-be graduates either decide to go wherever their first job takes them or else they decide where they want to be and pursue jobs in that region. If you are in the latter category, the beginning of your senior year is the time to decide where you want to be.

- If necessary, narrow down your list of dream employers based on geography, and strategize ways to contact key people in your dream companies.

- Join professional and mixed-industry organizations in your targeted geographic area (or transfer your student membership to the professional chapters). If it's not practical for you to attend meetings of these organizations, ask the membership chair for a membership list so you can start making contact with members.

- Meet with your adviser early in your senior year for an in-depth discussion of your career goals and ask for suggestions for people you should contact.

- Continue to maintain contact with professors, students, employers, guest speakers, and folks you've met through online networking efforts.

- Find out if your university or academic department has any kind of formal mentoring program and ask to be matched with a mentor. If no program exists, try to scout out a mentor on your own. Alumni often make especially good mentors.

- Fine-tune your list of potential network contacts and set a goal to contact a certain number of these each week or month. For the first half of your senior year, connecting with a few contacts each week should be sufficient. As the countdown to graduation begins in your final semester, you may want to try for at least one a day. Arrange to meet with as many contacts as possible, and always ask each one for more referrals. Send thank-you notes, and update your contacts regularly on your progress.

- Continue informational interviewing.

- Begin to contact people with whom you conducted informational interviews earlier in your college career to tell them that you are getting close to graduation and remain very interested in their organizations (see part 5).

- Enjoy your graduation ceremony with a big smile on your face, because if you've done all of the above, you are probably graduating with a job in hand. You are probably like the student dubbed "The Networking Queen" by Bill Carson, director of the Center for Career Development at Morgan State University: "The Networking Queen is a very recent college graduate who is a voracious researcher," Carson reports. "She asks questions of everyone she meets and follows up on *all leads*. She has been able to make significant entrées into circles that are traditionally closed to all but an elite few. She makes it known to all who met her that she is genuinely interested in learning more about her chosen profession and will go to great lengths to get the information and experience she needs. This approach has resulted in her ending up with many opportunities from which to choose. She is now in her second month of a management training program preparing for a career in corporate event planning and promotion." Be sure to write one more note to all your contacts telling them about your new job. And don't throw away any of your networking information; sometimes that first job doesn't work out, and you just might need to call upon your network again.

Networking Timetable for Established Job Seekers and Job Changers

For those who are already established in a career and are looking for a new job, the pace of networking varies considerably depending on whether you find yourself suddenly and unexpectedly unemployed or whether you're comfortably employed but have decided it's time to switch jobs or careers.

Let's first establish a couple of premises:

The savviest careerists maintain their networks at all times, even while happily employed. That way they don't have to scramble to build a network if they suddenly find themselves out of work.

The better developed your network is when you begin to seek a new job, the shorter your job search is likely to be.

Now, let's assume a fast-track pace for the unexpectedly unemployed; those who have the leisure of taking their time to find a new job or career can adapt this timetable at a less urgent clip. And let's assume the worst-case scenario—that the suddenly out-of-work job seeker does not have a well-established network.

- Brainstorm a list of potential contacts. Try to think of as many as you can.

- Realize that looking for a job should be almost a full-time job in itself. Plan to devote a significant portion of every day both to traditional open-market job-hunting activities (such as scanning and responding to ads and job postings) and to networking.

- Set a goal to connect with a certain number of contacts a day. The number will depend on the urgency of your job search and your financial situation. If it's very urgent, a goal of twenty contacts a day would not be unreasonable; if it's less urgent, five a day may fill the bill.

- Consider establishing or enhancing your visibility, personal branding, and online presence, as well as participating in online social/business networking venues (see chapters 15 to 17).

- Realize that even though there may be people on your list you'd be more comfortable writing to before you phone them, you may not have that luxury. The telephone may need to be your main networking tool when you're on a fast track; email is an option as well.

- Begin establishing contacts, keeping in mind the goals of seeking advice, more referrals, and face-to-face meetings.

Some of those meetings may be informational interviews, depending on your situation. Be sure to send thank-you notes to everyone who is even remotely helpful.

- Be on the lookout for events you can attend and organizations you can join to enhance your networking efforts, but don't make these your major focus (unless you are comfortably employed, in which case you can allow organization- and event-oriented networking to take priority over your daily routine of establishing new contacts). Squeeze in meetings and events whenever you can, and always try to give out business cards and resumes.

- At the end of your first two to three weeks of networking, go back and reconnect with your initial list of contacts. Tell them how you're doing and ask for any new ideas or referrals.

- If you are still unemployed at the end of the first month, begin the cycle again. Expand your list of contacts, based in part on new referrals your initial contacts have given you.

Lifelong Networking

If you haven't already picked up on the hint that networking over the long haul of your career is the best approach, let's make that clear right here. Ideally, networking that begins sometime while you're in

---

=={FOOT NOTE}==

Kate Wendleton, founder of the Five O'Clock Club, expands on the common wisdom that job hunting is a full-time job and that networking full time is extremely difficult when you're already employed. She suggests taking vacation days one day at a time, say every other Friday, and using those days for networking and interviews.

---

college and continues almost until retirement enables you to build a network of contacts, associates, and productive relationships. If networking is an ongoing process, you have a solid support system to fall back on when you need to find a job. You also have copious sources for perspectives and advice that will aid your career development, along with the people to talk to and receive support from when you have troubles on the job. After all, the average worker today is expected to change careers at least five times over the course of his working life, so a well-developed network can only make all the transitions easier.

So, in addition to all your regularly scheduled activities that present both organized and spontaneous networking opportunities, you might also want to set aside a certain chunk of time every week—a couple of hours perhaps—for individual networking. Write letters, make phone calls, send emails just to touch base with members of your network. The National Association of Female Executives advises going through your networking database every six months to see which people you haven't talked to recently. Regularly reconnect with your most valuable players.

=={FOOT NOTE}==

Summer can be a great time to network. Competition is minimal because job seekers assume that hiring decisions will be postponed until fall. While the assumption often proves correct, the groundwork for hiring can be laid in the summer—through effective networking. Just as parties and networking opportunities increase during the Christmas holidays, picnics, barbecues, beach parties, and outdoor sporting activities provide sizzling summertime networking occasions. Vacations can be planned around the possibility of relocating to another city. In addition, fiscal years often begin in June or July, making new hiring possible.

PART TWO

THE NITTY-GRITTY

OF NETWORKING

CHAPTER 7

THE PSYCHOLOGY OF
ASKING FOR ASSISTANCE

For many people, the most daunting aspect of networking is getting past the idea of asking for help. We don't want to seem as though we're begging or groveling or worse—using people. But the fact is that most people like to be asked for assistance. Being asked for advice flatters people and makes them feel important. Knowing that someone values their expertise inspires most people to go out of their way to help. People feel like heroes when they can help you achieve your career ambitions. Asking and helping create a bond between you and your network contact.

Benjamin Franklin said, "If you want to make a friend, let someone do you a favor." (I blatantly stole that quote from Chris Matthews, who cites Franklin in his book, *Hardball* (Touchstone, 1999), about how the game of politics is played.) The art of letting people do you favors, which Matthews contends is a key facet of political success, is also one of the best routes to effective networking. "Contrary to what many people assume," Matthews writes, "the most effective way to gain a person's loyalty is not to do him or her a favor, but to let that person do one for you." Matthews explains that when you enlist someone's aid, you are soliciting that person's investment in you and your success. The person not only feels good about helping you now, but also watches out for you in the future to make sure her faith in you was not misplaced. "Those who give you one helping hand very often make a habit of looking out for you further down the road," Matthews writes. "We tend naturally to remember the people we 'discover' along the way and seek to ensure that they prove us correct."

A significant part of networking is the process of simply talking to people about their work, learning what they like and don't like about it, and determining how and where you might fit into the same kind of work. If there's one thing people like discussing, it's their work. Work, after all, is a big part of our lives. And most people just love to talk about their jobs, which is why informational interviewing (part 4) is so effective. They are flattered to be asked advice. An effective way to solicit advice is to tell your contacts how much you value their opinion or expertise.

People also enjoy the sense of belonging they feel when you ask them to be part of your personal network. As long as you observe the rules of networking etiquette (chapter 10), you should not be perceived as a user.

All of this is not to say that networking should be a one-sided endeavor. You should share as much as you can with your network contacts. Allow your contact to determine how he can best be of assistance. Just don't be afraid to ask for that advice and assistance in the first place.

========================={FOOT NOTE}=========================

Don't assume that even those closest to you have an intimate grasp on exactly what kind of work you want to do and how you're qualified. You may have to spend some time with your contacts, perhaps over lunch or dinner, to give them a full understanding of what you're looking for and what you have to offer. You might feel silly handing your resume to your closest pals, but they can help you much more effectively with it than without it. Remember, too, that resumes hand-delivered to decision makers by members of your network carry significant added weight that can get you in the door.

CHAPTER 8

CONTACTS BEGET CONTACTS:
GETTING YOUR NETWORK TO WORK FOR YOU

You've probably heard the theory—subject of a Broadway play and a film—that between every ordinary person and a celebrity stand only six degrees of separation. The same could be said of networking. Because your network has the potential to expand exponentially, there may be six degrees of separation—give or take a few—between you and your next employer. That was roughly the phenomenon that one financial markets economist/analyst experienced. "Just out of graduate school, I hoped to work on Wall Street and had a few interviews set up," she relates. "No one actually had a job to offer. One person told me he had hired someone else, but he gave me a name to call. It was a government job and, with hiring freezes in many departments, I kept getting another name to call. Eventually, I ended up working in the White House for the president's economic adviser, all from following up on these referrals."

Earlier we noted that the average person potentially has 250 people in his network. But here's the real kicker. If you have a possible 250 people in your network, each person in your network also has a possible 250 people in his network—so your network has the

═══════════════════════[FOOT NOTE]═══════════════════════

Syndicated business columnist Mark McCormack recommends passing on "heads-up" information to members of your network, which might include news about the plans of a company that is your contact's competitor.

potential to grow almost endlessly. Some people actually have networks that vast; others neither have nor need such a massive support system. What's gratifying to know is that your network always has the potential to expand and, at any given time, you could have a lot of people invested in your success and helping you achieve it.

Your network can work for you even when you're not giving it your full attention, as career counselor Vic Snyder discovered. "[I left a job in] a technical college setting twelve years ago without a definite plan of what I wanted to do next," Snyder recalls. "Within a month a colleague contacted me to do consulting work in a vocational rehabilitation setting and that helped me decide to start my own private practice and consulting firm. My colleague knew that I was available through my network. It was working even though I didn't know it."

The Circle Paradigm

One way to look at how your network can work for you is to think of it as a series of overlapping circles. The innermost circle consists of your closest and most trusted friends and advisers. These are the

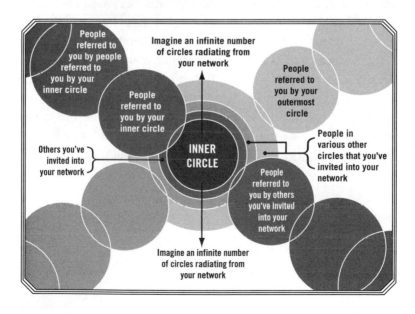

People referred to you by people referred to you by your inner circle

Imagine an infinite number of circles radiating from your network

People referred to you by your outermost circle

People referred to you by your inner circle

INNER CIRCLE

People in various other circles that you've invited into your network

Others you've invited into your network

People referred to you by others you've invited into your network

Imagine an infinite number of circles radiating from your network people you would turn to first in a time of crisis—say, if you lost your job. Working outward, the next circle is the people you don't know quite as well but do feel comfortable asking to be part of your network. Another circle is the people whom those in your inner circle refer you to. Another consists of the people referred by those in your outer circle. Further circles projecting outward are referrals made by your referrals. And so on . . .

The Theory of Weak Ties

While we may think of those in the inner circle as being the most helpful members of our networks, *Money* magazine reported on a study about networking, indicating that "weak ties may have more networking potential than strong ones. Intimate ties, those of families, close friends, and business partners, the study shows, create tight circles. Since acquaintances are people who move in other groups, they usually have more range."

Of those weak ties, according to writer Donna Clark, the type that may be of the greatest help to you is someone who has been contacted by a member of your network who has paved the way for you. The contacted person is expecting to hear from you. Writing in the *Business Journal* of Charlotte, North Carolina, Clark says this "target network" should also include hiring managers in companies you'd like to work for. A particularly effective way to network with hiring managers is through informational interviews (part 4). One survey respondent provided an extreme example of weak ties in networking, noting that she had learned of a job opportunity through "my boyfriend's friend's pastor's neighbor's friend!"

CHAPTER 9

NETWORKING FOR THE SHY AND INTIMIDATED

Think everyone who successfully networks must be a gregarious extrovert? The vast majority (70 percent) of job seekers surveyed for this book described themselves not as extremely outgoing but somewhere in between gregarious and shy. Most people possess some degree of shyness and unease with the idea of networking—and some are extremely uncomfortable with the idea. But there is hope for the very shy and intimidated. Just recognizing that few people are unreserved extroverts is half the battle, as Deborah Kubena learned. "I can sometimes be quite shy when it comes to approaching people I don't know," notes Kubena, a career counselor. "When I find I am hesitating to meet people, though, I remember that others are probably just as uncomfortable, and that [knowledge] gives me the courage to introduce myself first. Looking back, I can't remember a time when I've regretted making the first move." There were similarly no regrets for the client of Barbara Safani, president of Career Solvers, New York, New York: "I convinced a client who was uncomfortable with the idea of networking to attend a company alumni event," Safani says. "At the event she reconnected with a former colleague who put her back in touch with a former boss who happened to be looking for someone to fill an open position and hired her two weeks later." In addition to realizing you're far from the only one who is shy, here are some tips for the introverted networker:

- Start your networking efforts in settings where you know other participants, such as professional organizations.

- When trying to make one-on-one connections, such as for informational interviewing purposes, start with those you've been referred to by family members and close friends and work your way up to people with whom you have a common bond, such as fellow alumni of your college or high school.

- While you should avoid using as a crutch online methods of networking that keep you out of the social fray, the shy person can learn to get the most out of online discussion groups and web-based networking (as described in chapter 17).

- The pen is mightier than the phone, at least for the shy person. Writing to people you've been referred to is a superb way to introduce yourself and break the ice. Writing (or emailing) before phoning eases you into making network connections one-on-one. Writing gives you an opening for when you do call: "I'm calling to follow up on the letter I wrote you last week."

- When someone you know has referred you to someone you don't know, you can often ask your acquaintance to pave the way for you by calling and telling the stranger to expect to hear from you. That way, your phone call is made a little easier because you can say, "Hi, this is Sally Johnson. I believe Jeff Barnes told you I'd be calling."

- You will eventually have to pick up the phone and call people you don't know. You can write or email first, but sooner or later, you'll have to call. What is the best advice on how to go about it if you're shy? Just do it. Skip Haley, a self-proclaimed introvert interviewed on the CareerLab website by William Frank, has this to say about picking up the phone: "I absolutely hate it. But isn't it interesting—every time I do it, something good comes of it."

- Haley also suggests reminding yourself what will happen if you don't overcome your shyness and go out to events where networking takes place. "If you don't, you're not going to meet people. And if you don't meet people, you're not going to get a job."

- Plan out what you will say when you make phone contacts. You may even want to have a script in front of you, such as those in chapter 12. Just don't ever sound as though you're reading from a script. A bare-bones outline with key words will keep you from forgetting what you want to say while ensuring that you sound natural. Particularly when networking with people you know, begin with small talk about what's new with your contact before launching into your script.

- When you first attend a meeting of a professional organization, learn as much as you can about the group. Read the organization's publications. When attending events where networking is likely to take place, arrive a little early and introduce yourself to the organizer or host. You may even want to call ahead of time and explain that this is your first

---

[FOOT NOTE]

The buddy system is another effective defense against shyness at networking events. Pair up with a friend and make the rounds together. In an article on the buddy system, Clay Barrett told the story of Joan and Cathy, who worked in different industries and in different job roles but were both were laid off at about the same time. They met at a local networking group and hit it off immediately. Joan was shy but felt much more comfortable at the events with Cathy along. Meanwhile, Joan held Cathy accountable for following through on her networking efforts, previously her weak spot. Read the full article at www.quintcareers.com/networking_buddy_system.html.

---

time and you're trying to get the lay of the land. That way, you have someone who can introduce you to others at the event. If you stand near the door, advises Leslie Smith of the National Association for Female Executives, people may assume you are one of the organizers and introduce themselves to you. Another trick, says speaker and author Mariette Durack Edwards, is to ask someone at the check-in desk to suggest a member who can introduce you to others.

- Even if you're feeling uneasy, try to smile and project enthusiasm and confidence. Networking for the shy and introverted is something of a performance. Sometimes you have to be a good actor. Even shy individuals are capable of acting like confident people. You simply have to step into your self-assured persona. You can slip back into the shy identity you're more comfortable with after you've accomplished what you need to. Does this basically amount to faking it—pretending to be someone you're not? Probably not. You're just using the tools within you to get a job done. They may not be tools you enjoy using every day, but they are tools you can employ when you need them.

- Be aware of your surroundings and adapt your approach to the setting. If you're at an event where networking is the main focus, you can adopt your go-getter persona. But if it's a social event, hang back a bit and wait for appropriate

---

=={FOOT NOTE}==

One good strategy is to redirect your shyness toward helping others have a productive time, says the National Association for Female Executives. If you pretend it's your party and your responsibility to ensure everyone's enjoyment, you can relegate your shyness to the back burner.

---

openings before you make networking contacts. Look for people who are by themselves. They are likely to be just as shy as you and would love to be approached. Making eye contact with people throughout the room and smiling will encourage them to gravitate to you. Turn the tables on your shy self by making it your mission to make others feel at home and relaxed.

- Be sure you're up on current events when you attend an affair where networking may take place. Topical issues—including sports—are always great icebreakers (as long as they're not too controversial). It also doesn't hurt to have read some of the latest books and seen current movies (or at least read the reviews). Bone up on current issues in your field as well by reading trade and professional journals.

- Prepare some leading questions that will break the ice and get people to talk. Be curious and interested. Ask people lots of questions about themselves and their jobs. They'll love answering you, and you'll have less talking to do. But you'll still make a good connection because you gave someone a chance to talk about herself. Many of the questions suggested in chapter 22 for informational interviews work well in this situation, especially from the sections "All about Your Interviewee's Job" and "About Your Interviewee's Career Path."

- Many of us are shy about networking because we fear rejection. Ask yourself: What's the worst thing that could happen? Someone you meet could be standoffish; someone you ask for advice may hesitate to give it. Whatever you do, don't take it personally. Just tell yourself that it's no big deal and move on.

- If your biggest fear is not that others will react badly but that you will say or do something stupid, lighten up. Everyone, even the most polished professionals, makes a silly and embarrassing mistake now and then. Learn to laugh off your gaffes.

- Set goals for yourself. Whether it's making five phone calls a day, exchanging three business cards at an event, or adding one new person a day to your network, you will be more likely to rise above your shyness if you set and meet goals. Take a break in between each step toward your goal, and reward yourself with a little treat when you meet each goal—eating a favorite food, soaking in a hot bath, renting a good movie—whatever feels like a reward to you. And don't give up when you don't meet your goals.

- Celebrate your successes. It's almost a sure bet that you'll have more successes than you expect and more successes than failures. Bask in your triumphs and let the momentum encourage you to be a little less shy the next time.

CHAPTER 10

NETWORKING ETIQUETTE

"People don't mind being used," writes Chris Matthews in *Hardball*. "What they mind is being taken for granted." Author and public speaker Jeff Roberts describes how his wife was left feeling used and betrayed by a thoughtless job seeker. "My wife, a human resources professional, was burned once by someone who used her in networking," Roberts relates. "The experience left her extremely cautious in helping others. A fellow employee lost her job and asked my wife if she knew anyone in field X. My wife went out of her way to set this coworker up with a friend prominent in the field who offered assistance. The coworker never spoke one word in appreciation for the lead or even talked with my wife again until she needed another lead. I urge all people using networking to remember the relationship dimensions of the experience. Make sure that you bend over backward to let the people know of your appreciation for their assistance." Beyond the simple courtesy of showing your appreciation (see sample thank-you notes in part 5), other aspects of networking etiquette are worth keeping in mind:

- **Know your purpose for networking.** It sounds obvious, but job seekers waste their contacts' time when they don't really know what they want to do, where they want to work, or how the contact might be helpful to them. A survey respondent pointed to "lost opportunities of speaking with others and not having a clear focus on what they wanted to achieve—thus, they were not able to brand themselves nor move to the next stage." Think about what employers you ultimately want to target through networking; strive to list fifteen to twenty companies for starters. Consider through which venues—such as professional organizations and events—you can best identify the contacts that will lead you to your targeted employers. Also think about cultivating network contacts among vendors who sell to your target companies and customers who buy from them, associations the companies might belong to, former employees, distributors, competitors, and business-service firms—printers, realtors, bankers, and ad agencies, for example, that the companies interact with. Set specific, strategic goals at each venue for the kinds of contacts you want to make and how you will approach them.

- **Do your homework.** Don't ask your contacts questions that could easily be answered by doing a little basic research. The more you know about your contacts' companies and backgrounds, the more impressed they will be with you. Also be in the know about latest industry news and trends and be prepared to converse knowledgeably on several newsy topical areas you know will interest your contacts.

- **Don't act desperate.** The smell of fear emanating from a networking job seeker can be a real turn-off. Your contacts will be much more willing to help someone who is confident and capable than someone groveling, whining, and desperate. Don't forget that as high a priority as it is to you your job search is not so to most of your network contacts. Be positive and upbeat. A survey respondent notes that networking failures tend to revolve around unwillingness or half-heartedness of the networking attempt, while success revolves around enjoying the event and showing happiness. Smiling and making eye contact will generate an aura of competence and approachability. "If you have fun, they'll have fun," writes William Frank in his CareerLab website. "If they have fun, they'll like you. If they like you, they're more likely to help you or hire you."

- **Listen.** When a contact is kind enough to offer you advice, listen attentively. Don't monopolize the conversation. Don't rush through the conversation and start to seek out the next person before you're finished with your current conversation partner. When you write your contact a thank-you note, include something that tells your contact you listened.

- **Respect your contact's time.** Don't drop into a contact's office uninvited, and when you call a current or prospective member of your network, always ask if he has time to talk. Even when the answer is yes, make your conversation brief and to the point. Also, be aware of time zones if you contact people in other parts of the country. A sleepy Californian would not appreciate a call made at 9 A.M. New York time. When the situation allows, bide your time before launching into networking talk. An overeager networker that A. Charles Kovacs observed had not learned this lesson. "As the passenger sat down in his seat and introduced himself to the woman in the next seat, he began explaining his destination and activity in France setting up a new international vacation resort in the West Indies," reports Kovacs, who is director of the Office of Career Services at Bates College, Lewiston, Maine. "Before the gentleman could complete the details of his projected venture, the woman was pushing her interests, candidacy, and qualifications. That turned him totally off, and the rest of the flight he sat in stony silence. Moral of the story: patience in making your pitch."

- **Ask for help in small doses.** Don't burden your contact with overwhelming requests for help and advice. Ask more questions than favors. You can always ask for more at a later time.

- **Get permission** before using a network contact's name to approach another prospective contact. Similarly, when you're scouting for new members of your network, tell prospective contacts how you got their names. Honor any requests for confidentiality.

- **Be careful with your use of the word *networking*.** While it's generally quite effective to ask people if they'd be willing to be part of your personal network, some people have grown weary of being networked. Unless you are attending a function specifically earmarked for networking, it's best not to advertise the fact that that is what you are doing. Instead, think of yourself as making connections, building relationships, and seeking advice.

- **Don't be pushy and aggressive.** Be sensitive to just how much a contact is willing to do for you, and don't push beyond that limit. "I have clients who have pestered contacts so regularly that they have been told never to make contact again," notes Mina Patel, employment liaison coordinator at Auckland University of Technology in New Zealand. Be persistent but not annoying.

- **Never criticize anything or anyone when you're networking.** This tip comes from one of my former Stetson University students, Alissa Slaven. "This is one of the first impressions people have of you, and it will stick in their head that you're a negative person," Slaven notes. "Also, you never know how

---

[FOOT NOTE]

A critical component of any networker's etiquette kit should be breath mints. Don't leave home without them.

they truly feel about something—for example, if you poke fun at a lady wearing an oversized flowered hat, it might remind your potential contact of her mother or grandmother."

- **Remember that networking is a two-way street.** The idea of reciprocity is perhaps the most important aspect of networking etiquette. "The best, most memorable networkers are more interested in learning about how they can help you than in what you can do for them," states Andrea Joldrichsen, associate director of full-time placement and chemical engineering, University of Toledo, Toledo, Ohio. Offer your help to your contacts and supply needed information whenever possible.

Writing in the *Arizona Business Gazette*, Mark McCormack talks about attending Jaycee events where many attendees were there solely for what they could take from the group—contacts, business cards, sales leads. By offering to organize a golf event for the group, McCormack built a reputation as a giver instead of a taker. Recruitment specialist Jim Stroud recommends being the first member of a networking partnership to offer something—an idea, information, an introduction—to your contacts.

"Cultivate a habit of being interested in the needs of others," writes Henry Neils, president and founder of Assessment.com. If you can enter into networking with a positive, giving attitude, you will succeed by helping others succeed. "I love meeting people," says Terri Ferrara, a job search expert in Traverse City, Michigan, with Summit View Career Coaching. "So, wherever I am standing around and there is someone I don't know, it is my aim to get to know that person so I can appreciate her strengths and uniqueness. It may be standing in a grocery line, being friendly to clerks waiting on me, and so on." Career transition consultant and author Billie R. Sucher cites the unexpected returns: "Networking is not about getting; it is about giving. And you never know how it will come back to you," she says. "A couple of years ago my daughter and I attended the Tina Turner concert in Kansas City," Sucher recalls. "During intermission, I went to the powder room, and there stood a young woman sobbing at the sink. She was really upset. I approached her and gently inquired, 'Are you okay?' She immediately blurted out, 'No, I'm not okay. I got fired from my job today, and I am NOT OKAY!' I expressed my concerns, and we chatted for a few moments until she calmed down. I offered her my business card, sharing something like 'if there's ever anything I can do to help, just let me know.' The very next week she called me to discuss my services and to thank me 'for caring about someone you didn't even know.'"

When a contact gives you help, information, or advice, plan to respond with the same as soon as you can. "Who can I connect you with?" is a welcome offer, says Thomas Power of ecademy.com. And when you do offer help, follow through with your promises.

College students should be especially aware of the give-and-take aspect of networking, as they are the population most likely to forget. Steve Rothberg, founder of CollegeRecruiter.com, tried to add networking functions to his site but failed because the college students who sought help and advice neglected to reciprocate for their contacts. Rothberg explains that his company set up an interactive, email-based discussion list where tens of thousands of students and recent graduates were encouraged to post their career-related questions and answers to questions posted by others. The students and grads posted lots of questions and requests for help, but Rothberg says, "we had almost no one posting answers or offers to assist." The young networkers, Rothberg says, became "indignant when no one offered them a job and all they received back over the coming days were resumes and requests for assistance for other job seekers." Rothberg laments that the job seekers couldn't . . . understand that what the others were doing that was so upsetting to them was exactly what they were doing themselves."

CHAPTER 11

SELL THE SIZZLE: ADVERTISING THE PRODUCT (YOU)

For many people, one of the more intimidating aspects of networking is the marketing and sales element. Building relationships is wonderfully rewarding, but those relationships will prove all the more fruitful to your career if you can also sell your network contacts on how wonderful you are. Most of us like to talk about ourselves—or at least we are less uncomfortable talking about ourselves than we are talking about other topics. When you network, you always tread a fine line between the confident and the boastful—the scintillating raconteur relating fascinating tales of accomplishment and the crashing bore who alienates everyone with his bombast.

Your Unique Selling Proposition

The first trick to selling yourself is to identify the one thing about you that makes you unique among job seekers. What's the one thing you do better than anyone else? In advertising, the one thing that makes a product better than any other is its Unique Selling Proposition. Is it easy to come up with one thing you do better than anyone else? Nope. But identifying something about yourself that makes you especially appealing to employers will help not only with your networking efforts but also with the entire marketing campaign that comprises your job search. Once you've identified your Unique Selling Proposition, you can make it the centerpiece of three types of one-on-one networking communications: the sound bite, the commercial, and the infomercial.

Note that these types of communication are often referred to as elevator speeches or elevator pitches.

THE SOUND BITE

The sound bite, a concept introduced by Brian Krueger in his book *The College Grad Job Hunter* (Adams, 2008), is a very short introduction of yourself used in situations where you are meeting a lot of people and probably not spending a great deal of time with any one of them. Events specifically designed for networking are ideal for the sound bite, which lasts about fifteen to twenty seconds and may or may not be the prelude to a lengthier conversation. The trick is to make your sound bite so intriguing that people will want to spend more time talking with you. The sound bite also might be incorporated into an initial phone conversation with a prospective new member of your network.

At its most basic level, the sound bite's structure is this:

Hi, my name is _____. I'm in the _____ field, and I'm looking to _____.

The last blank would be filled in with your current career aspiration, whether to stay within your field and move up or to move into a different career.

A college student or new graduate might add the following to the basic structure:

Hi, my name is _____. I will be graduating/I just graduated from _____ with a degree in _____. I'm looking to _____.

You can stick with the sound bite's basic structure and see where it takes you, or you can add an element of intrigue by incorporating your Unique Selling Proposition. Let's look, for example, at how a conversation might go that starts with an intriguing sound bite:

Networker #1: Hi, my name is Carmen Southwick. I deal in dreams.

Networker #2: How do you do that?

Networker #1: I'm a wedding planner. I plan dream weddings for couples. I've been working for myself, but I'd like to get in with one of the big resorts that puts on weddings.

As you can imagine, the ensuing conversation now has considerable potential. Let's look at another example:

Networker #1: Hi, my name is Ned Peters. I turn animals into smiles.

Networker #2: How so?

Networker #1: I manage a pet store and love to watch children's eyes light up when I put a little animal in their hands. I'm training to use pet therapy in hospitals and nursing homes and hope to break into that field.

And one more:

Networker #1: Hi, my name is Betty Joiner. I train future leaders.

Networker #2: This I've got to hear about.

Networker #1: I'm a teacher! I love shaping the minds of the next generation, but I'm also interested in getting into corporate training.

The concern, of course, with the intriguing sound bite is that you'll sound corny or hokey. And, in fact, chances are you will. But you will also hook your conversation partner into finding out more about you. You just have to decide whether or not you're comfortable with incorporating an intriguing line into your sound bite; if not, go for a more basic approach. One way to test the effect of your sound bite is to try it out on members of your inner circle.

THE COMMERCIAL

The commercial is a longer version of the sound bite and can be used in networking situations in which you have more time to talk about yourself, such as when you are having lunch with a contact or visiting in her office. It's also a good response when you're conducting an informational interview and the interviewee turns the tables and starts asking questions about you. The commercial can also piggyback on top of the sound bite; you start out with the sound bite, and your conversation partner asks you to tell more about yourself, so you segue into the commercial. This introduction is typically thirty to sixty seconds long and contains more about your background, qualifications, and skills than the sound bite does. Obviously, you don't want your commercial to sound memorized. But you are, after all, talking about yourself, so the material should not be hard to remember. It helps to write it out first (outline form is fine), then read it over a few times and practice saying it without reading or memorizing it. It's not a big deal if you forget a detail, as long as you remember the main points you want to get across. Here are a couple of samples:

=======[FOOT NOTE]=======

If you feel too corny using your hook in your sound bite, consider writing it under your name on your name tag. People will likely ask you to explain what it means, thus opening up conversation possibilities. Learn more about unusual name tag uses at http://hellomynameisscott.com/landing.aspx, the website of Scott Ginsburg, who has carved an entire business out of the fact that he wears his name tag all the time. He had been wearing it for more than 2,400 days when last I checked.

"Hi, my name is Michaela Shaw. In my job as database controller for _____ company, where I worked for _____ years, I was drawn to the field of information systems. I enjoyed the challenge of learning new technologies, and I loved implementing the systems management training I received while working with the Hewlett-Packard board test system. It was as if a spark ignited and suddenly I knew what I wanted to do. I began to focus my efforts on obtaining additional training in computer information systems. In my _____ classes, I led a research team in _____ subject, and . . . (other experience). My academic work has strengthened my communications skills, which were extremely important in my job as _____. I have also worked with the latest technologies in my classes. For example, I helped design a database interface application in Visual Basic for one of my school's programs. Whenever I have been assigned a project, I have done my best to see it through to top-notch completion. I am prepared to take the next step in my career."

"Hi, my name is Mateo Santiago. My background has centered around preparing myself to be the most well-rounded marketing professional possible. I have specifically prepared for a career in marketing by taking competitive undergraduate classes and by gaining invaluable real-world experience. To improve my written communication skills, I completed four upper-division English classes in addition to the two core classes required of business majors. Since many Texas businesses work with people of Hispanic origin, I chose to enhance my desirability and versatility as a potential employee by acquiring a Spanish minor. I have also acquired real-world experience to prepare for the business world, including travel abroad, internships, and entrepreneurial opportunities. While interning with a private organization in Ecuador this past summer, I developed a fifteen-page marketing plan, composed in Spanish, that recommended more effective ways in which this company could promote its services. I also traveled abroad on two other occasions in which I researched the indigenous culture of the Mayan Indians in Todos Santos, Guatemala, and participated in a total language immersion program in San José, Costa Rica. In addition to my travel and internship experience, I also obtained considerable professional sales training as a result of my own entrepreneurial pursuits. During this past summer, I telemarketed for Riella Tire Supply of West Texas, a work experience that prompted me to develop my conflict-resolution and personal selling skills. I have also established and maintained two businesses—Santiago Lawn Service and Full Throttle Auto Detailing, which gave me useful real-world experience with cold door-to-door sales calls and relationship selling. As you can see, I am committed to succeed as a marketing professional."

THE INFOMERCIAL

The infomercial is meant for extended networking situations where you are spending a significant chunk of time with a contact. Perhaps you hit it off with someone in your field on a five-hour cross-country airplane flight. Or you are rooming with a stranger at a professional conference who promises to be a helpful contact. The infomercial may not come into play very often, but when it does, you have the opportunity to really sell yourself. The infomercial builds on the commercial. Instead of extending your commercial sales pitch, however, the infomercial consists primarily of preparing for questions your networking partner is likely to pose after hearing about your background. The truly interested network contact asks these questions so she can better assist you. Among the questions you should be prepared to respond to as part of your infomercial are:

- How did you get into this field?

- How would you describe your ideal job?

- What goals do you have for five years from now?

- What are your strengths and weaknesses?

- Do you plan to obtain further education or training in pursuit of your goals?

- In what geographic area do you want to work?

Your infomercial presentation can also include your observations about interesting trends and events in your field.

CHAPTER 12

HOW NETWORKING REALLY WORKS: A WEEK IN THE LIFE OF A NETWORKER

To illustrate how networking really works and show what wording your letters and phone calls might contain, let's look back at our friend John from chapter 1, the systems analyst ready to change careers. John had the opportunity to teach a class in systems analysis one semester at a community college, and he discovered that he especially enjoyed designing the curriculum. He got a kick out of planning his syllabus and setting up his entire course on a website. He decided that instructional design was a field he'd really like to get into, especially since he was weary of his current career. As Guy Felton suggests on his networking website, John made it clear to each contact exactly what he was asking for, and those requests are indicated in bold in the following. Here's how John's first week of networking went.

Monday

After work, John attends a meeting of the Association of Instructional Designers. During the social hour, John mingles with the instructional design professionals, using the sound bite technique:

"Hi, my name is John Randall. I'm a systems analyst, but I'm really interested in getting into your field."

John goes on to describe how much he'd enjoyed designing his own course and how he feels his current career relates to instructional design. John also asks questions about his contacts' jobs—how they got into the field, what they enjoy about it, what exactly their role is. He asks questions to keep the conversation flowing. He ensures that his questions are open-ended—not yes-or-no questions—like these suggested by career expert Louise Kursmark: "Who do you know at XYZ Corp?" (Not, "Do you know anyone at XYZ Corp?") "Who do you know who's involved in manufacturing in Greenville?" "If you were in my shoes, who would you talk to next?" "What are the most active professional associations you belong to?" "Tell me about the business culture in [name of targeted city]." "What's your take on how the new state regulations will affect the transportation industry?" "You know so many people in the _____ industry; I'd really respect your suggestions about which agencies I should approach."

Almost everyone John talks to is friendly and receptive and offers him a business card (and John asks for one if a contact neglects to offer him a card). He closes several conversations by asking **who else he should be talking to about getting into the field** and jots down several names. By the end of the evening, he has a good feel for the key area employers in the instructional design field, and he also asks his contacts for **the names of key people at those companies.**

Tuesday

John organizes the business cards and list of names he's collected from the meeting. The first person he calls is Della, who seemed particularly friendly and interested in helping John break into instructional design. John begins the conversation like this:

> "Hi, this is John Randall. I met you at the meeting of the Association of Instructional Designers last night and really enjoyed talking with you and hearing your advice. Do you have a few minutes? [Waits for response.] As you may recall, I'm interested in breaking into instructional design and would love to get together with you briefly and hear some more of that great advice." (John is careful to tell everyone with whom he tries to arrange a meeting

that he needs only a few minutes of their time, but he's also poised to ask questions over the phone in case the contact can't spare time for a one-on-one meeting.)

Della suggests that they meet for coffee the next day. John plans for his face-to-face meeting with Della (and the other meetings he will have in the future) by coming up with some questions he wants to ask. (The list of one hundred questions for informational interviews, especially those in the "Seeking General Advice and Referrals from Your Interviewee" and "Seeking Advice If You Are a Career Changer" sections in chapter 22, is a good place to begin.) Later, John looks at his list of people whom organization members suggested he contact. Since he hasn't met any of these people, he decides it might be a good idea to write to some of them to introduce himself before calling.

(The letter on the next page is a good example of the standard business-letter format. Other sample letters in the book are examples of content only, not format. Refer back to this example if you need to know how to set up your letter.)

Wednesday

John has his meeting with Della over coffee. She is just as congenial as she was Monday night. She suggests a couple of courses that John might take to bolster his instructional design skills, and she gives him some additional names of people to contact. **John has brought some copies of his resume and tells Della to feel free to distribute them to appropriate contacts in her network.** John also asks Della to keep him in mind if she hears of any appropriate job leads for him. Della reveals that she is close friends with a hiring manager at one of the companies John is interested in. **He asks Della for a direct introduction to the hiring manager** and Della says she'll see what she can do. As a next step, John tells Della that he will follow up on her suggestions and let her know next week how things are going. John goes home to write more letters and phone people on his growing

John H. Randall
1545 Elmont Street
Kansas City, MO 64114
(816) 555-3829

November 30, 2007

Mr. C. Benjamin Stevenson
Curriculum Design Dept.
InstructoSource
555 Fifth Avenue
Kansas City, MO 64100

Dear Mr. Stevenson:

Barry Bartram, whom I met at a recent meeting of the Association of Instructional Designers, suggested I contact you about my interest in entering the instructional design field. I'm currently a systems analyst, but I did some instructional design as the result of teaching a class at Indian Mills Community College. I am intrigued by the field, especially the possibilities that Web-based instruction presents.

I would be very grateful for any suggestions you might have.

I'd like to contact you in the near future to "pick your brain." I won't take much of your time and will greatly appreciate any advice you can offer.

Sincerely,

John Randall

John Randall

list of contacts. Some of the people he calls agree to meet with him; others give him still more names. In the course of one conversation, John discovers a mutual interest in golf with his contact, Greg, who invites John to play a round the following Sunday. John also takes some time on Wednesday to write a thank-you note to Della (see part 5). He tucks a magazine article that he thinks would interest Della into the envelope.

Thursday

John has lunch with his good friend, Sid, a member of his inner circle. John tells Sid about his plans to change careers and about his networking efforts. It turns out that Sid knows someone in a management position at a software company that often hires instructional designers. Sid gives John contact information for his friend, Dave. **John asks if Sid can "pre-sell" him to Dave.** Sid gets out his cell phone, calls Dave right away, and sings John's praises. Dave suggests that John call him at home that evening. John begins the conversation like this:

> "Hi, my name is John Randall. Sid Jackson suggested I contact you. Have I caught you at a good time? [Waits for response.] I'm exploring the instructional design field, and Sid tells me that your company has an instructional design component. I'm not quite at the point of looking for a job in the field, but I wondered if I could snag a few minutes of your time so I could tell you what I'm doing, ask you a few questions about your company, and get your perspective on what it takes to be an instructional designer."

Dave invites John to come to his office the next week. John immediately calls Sid to tell him about the successful conversation he had with Dave and to thank Sid for the productive referral. John even sneaks in a question about whether Sid knows anyone else in Dave's company or in instructional design. Sid says he'll think about whom he might know and get back to John.

Friday

John figures that Mr. Stevenson, the referral he wrote to on Tuesday, has probably received his letter by now, so it's time to follow up with a phone call. He begins the conversation like this:

> "Hi, Mr. Stevenson, this is John Randall calling. I wrote you a letter earlier this week. Am I keeping you from anything? [Waits for response.] As you recall, I wrote to see if I could get your advice about getting into the instructional design field. Do you have any suggestions for me?"

Mr. Stevenson explains that he does not have time for a meeting, but John is ready with a few quick questions to ask over the phone. Mr. Stevenson suggests a number of companies that John should consider, and he also gives John several more names. After hanging up, John writes Mr. Stevenson a thank-you note and strategizes about how he will contact his new referrals. Figuring that he might be able to get his feet wet in the field by taking on an instructional-design project on a consulting basis, **John plans to ask some of them if they know of any new projects in instructional design or problems that firms in the field may be experiencing**.

Saturday

John spends some time organizing his networking information and growing set of contacts. He makes plans for the following week's networking activities. John also uses his downtime on Saturday to read trade publications in the instructional design field, as well as current business publications. He knows that keeping current on developments in the field will help grease the wheels of his conversations with contacts, and the tidbits he picks up from business publications will enable him to offer timely insights and ideas to the people he talks to—so his encounters aren't totally one-sided.

Sunday

John enjoys his golf game with Greg. The hours on the golf course enable John to get to know Greg better and obtain significant advice from him. He also gets some new referral names from Greg. **He asks Greg which executive recruiters work with the companies John is most interested in, and Greg fills him in.** John's networking thus far has yielded the information that a key vice president in the instructional-design field is also a golfer, and **John finds out from Greg where the vice president plays golf.** After returning home, John writes Greg a thank-you letter and offers to host Greg at his local golf course soon. John makes plans to play a round at the club the target vice president uses in the hope John can talk to him there.

By Sunday night, John is beginning to realize, thanks to the advice of the many people he's talked to over the last week, that he will probably need to obtain a little more training before he can make the transition into instructional design. He knows, however, that his network is well established and that he can continue to build on it while keeping his current job and taking some night courses. He makes plans to reconnect with all the people who have given him advice to update them on his progress and see if they have any further suggestions. He is looking forward to his meeting with Sid's friend, Dave, in the coming week. **John plans to ask Dave for advice on how to approach Dave's company, which is one of John's targeted employers.**

Thus, we've seen through John's experience that networking is especially effective when you ask clearly for what you want each contact to do for you. Among the specifics you can ask for:

- Distribution of your resume to appropriate contacts

- Names of key people at targeted employers

- Advice on how to approach a targeted employer

- A direct introduction to a hiring manager

- Having a contact pave the way or "pre-sell" you to a key person

- Information about new projects you might be able to tackle and problems you might be able to solve at targeted companies

- Information on where a key person plays golf or otherwise spends his leisure time

- Information on which executive recruiters key companies employ

- Advice on how to launch a new career

CHAPTER 13

NETWORKING IN THE DIVERSE WORK WORLD

The increasing diversity of the workplace mandates a commitment to ethnic and cultural sensitivity, which also applies to networking. Underrepresented groups face special challenges and obstacles in the world of networking. And even those facing no unusual obstacles must be aware of how various groups view networking. One gentleman who wrote to me while I was researching this book pointed out that people of Asian origin tend to look with disdain on the concept of networking because they view the practice as akin to "using" people. An African American woman told me she had much networking success in obtaining referrals and interviews but racism and discrimination had kept her from being hired. While I make no attempt to offer a comprehensive guide to networking for those in underrepresented groups, I offer some tips. Virtually all groups have networking organizations available to them that are specifically earmarked for their situation or ethnicity. Clubs and organizations are available for women, African Americans, Latinos, Asians, the disabled, older workers, and many others, some of which are listed in the Resources section. In addition, members of these organizations often particularly benefit from having mentors, especially mentors with the same backgrounds. It's always helpful to learn about how someone like you has overcome some of the same obstacles you face. Some additional tips:

- George Fraser is widely regarded as the networking guru for African Americans. Author of *Success Runs in Our Race: The Complete Guide to Effective Networking in the Black*

Community (Amistad, 2004) and *Race for Success: The Ten Best Business Opportunities for Blacks in America* (Harper, 1999), Fraser writes, "It is vital for African Americans to network for their common good. In spite of media images to the contrary, we are historically a race of successful people, and we have always been a successful people, even when in chains." Fraser also asserts that most of his ideas on networking for African Americans can also benefit other minority groups. He suggests that members of minority groups must support each other. His advice is helpful not only to members of all underrepresented groups, but also to networkers in general.

Fraser and others believe strongly in ethnocentric networks; for African Americans that means Afrocentric networks, such as churches, which have traditionally helped to hold African American communities together. Another type of Afrocentric group, recommended by Andrea Wright in *Essence* magazine, is the black alumni association. If your school doesn't have one of these associations, consider forming one.

- Groups that are not only Afrocentric but women-centered as well can help African American women's careers. Writing in *Black Enterprise* magazine (which is another fantastic

=={FOOT NOTE}==

If you're networking in the international arena, be aware that other cultures have different attitudes than Americans about networking at social events and business-card exchanges. Raise your cultural sensitivity by reading up on the customs of other cultures and the acceptability of typically American networking activities. You may even want to take a course or attend a seminar to enhance your awareness of international networking practices.

resource on networking for everyone, not just African Americans), Carolyn Odom Steele declares, "No longer reluctant to leverage our clout or tap into high-powered contacts, these loosely defined, essentially structureless networks are effectively influencing the positions of African American women across the nation."

- Attend black-sponsored events. Invite African Americans— and not just a token few—to attend your events.

- Starting your own networking group can be especially helpful for women, as well as minorities. Women's networking groups have grown significantly in recent years, partly in the theory that women are at their greatest comfort levels when interacting with other women. Communication theorists such as Deborah Tannen, author of *You Just Don't Understand* (Harper, 2001), suggest that women are better listeners than men; thus, groups providing mutual support work well for women.

- Black fraternities and sororities offer "the post-college networking and support systems that white college graduates have traditionally found in groups like the Jaycees and Kiwanis," writes James Tobin in the *Detroit News*. The major black fraternities are Kappa Alpha Psi, Alpha Phi Alpha, Omega

====================[FOOT NOTE]====================

George Fraser offers these tips for non-African Americans
when they network with African Americans:

- Don't generalize about African Americans as a race or assume all have the same tastes; get to know them as individuals.

- Don't assume all thirty million African Americans know each other or have universal knowledge of black popular culture.

Psi Phi, Phi Beta Sigma, and Iota Phi Theta. The sororities are Alpha Kappa Alpha, Delta Sigma Theta, Zeta Phi Beta, and Sigma Gamma Rho.

- Don't worry about whether you're bothering people when you network. Columnist Niki Scott encourages women in particular to be persistent, since their natural tendency is to fear that they are annoying people when they seek advice and assistance.

- Learn to play golf. More and more members of underrepresented groups are discovering just how much networking occurs during golf games. "I never thought I would learn to play golf," says University of Central Florida cooperative education coordinator Lara Cegala, "but I have so I could network with employers on the golf course. It's the best way to get their attention."

- Networking is especially important for older workers because jobs at the senior levels are the least likely to be advertised. It's important to fight the perception that your skills and knowledge might not be on the cutting edge. Stay up to date with technological trends and be sure to demonstrate your savvy when you converse with network contacts.

  The AARP, American Association of Retired Persons, offers seminars on postcareer planning, workforce reentry, and resume writing for older workers. The seminars provide not only information but also networking opportunities. Call the national headquarters at 800-424-3410 (or visit their website at www.aarp.org) to find out about sessions near you.

- Young networkers should start as early as possible. Always view summer jobs and internships as opportunities to network.

- Among some good networking resources for Hispanics is His-panicBusiness.com (www.HispanicBusiness.com), which is associated with *Hispanic Business* magazine and offers networking events to the Hispanic community. See Resources, pages 205–6 for more.

- Tip for former military personnel: Retired military personnel are no strangers to networking, notes Pamela McBride in *Black Enterprise* magazine. It's what they do every day to get things done in the military. While networking comes naturally to former service people, they are accustomed to a sheltered, structured environment. Try to build a civilian network before you leave the service, and don't take rejection personally as you network outside military circles.

- Tip for the downsized or fired worker: Take a little time to step back and decide what you want your next career move to be and what you have to offer when you start networking, advises Ann Meier in *Training & Development* magazine. It's not enough simply to tell the world you're available the moment you're handed that pink slip. You need at least a few days to compose yourself.

CHAPTER 14

DUCKS IN A ROW:
KEEPING TRACK OF YOUR NETWORK

You can maximize your network's effectiveness if you organize your list of contacts. That way you can keep track of whom you've contacted and when. With a good system, you can have at your fingertips contact names and information that you might otherwise forget. Plan to weed through your organizational system periodically to update contact information and place in an inactive area of your system those members of your network with whom you are no longer in touch.

Business Cards

Since business cards are the essential tools of networking, they can also form the basis of an organizational system. At the most rudimentary level, you could simply alphabetize the cards you collect and wrap a rubber band around them. The next step might be purchasing a file box especially made for business cards.

Some people like to keep their business cards in a binder. If that method appeals to you, you can purchase a business-card binder, which is usually about the width of a business card and fits nicely into an attaché case or purse. If you prefer a three-ring binder, you can get special plastic sheets for business cards. These three-hole-punched, 8½-x-11-inch sheets can hold ten business cards. Another alternative is to lay ten business cards on the glass of a photocopier in the configuration of an 8½-x-11-inch sheet (two across and five down), photocopy them all onto a page, and three-hole-punch the pages.

It's now also possible to digitize business card information with a piece of hardware called a business card reader and retain these contact details on your computer.

Index Cards

If you desire a system that is as low-tech as a business card but that has more space to record information about each contact, you might use file cards, which typically come in 3-x-5-inch, 4-x-6-inch, and 5-x-8-inch sizes, ruled or unruled, and in many colors. File boxes are also available for the cards. Consider attaching business cards to the index cards and writing additional information about each contact in the extra space.

Computerized Systems

Those who prefer a more high-tech system that is easier to update may want to organize their contacts in a spreadsheet program, such

[FOOT NOTE]

When attending network events, use the backs of business cards to jot down information about each person who gave you one. Your notes will help you remember your contacts and enable you to converse intelligently with them the next time you meet. Career coach Carl Reid also suggests making contacts feel important by taking a few seconds to look at their business cards when offered. He advises tucking your business cards into virtually anything sent by mail—bills, thank-you notes, greeting cards— as well as giving out cards when asking contacts for referrals.

Don't forget to take a pen to these events. You'll get basic contact information by exchanging business cards, but you'll occasionally encounter someone without cards or you will wish to expand on the card's information by jotting down common interests, birthdays, and other notes that will help you make the most of each contact.

as Lotus 1-2-3 or Microsoft Excel. The spreadsheet could have columns for each contact's name, address, phone numbers, fax number, email address, where you met or who referred you, the date you met, your follow-up communications, and comments about the contact and how he helped you. See sample spreadsheet entries on page 102. You might instead prefer a database program, such as Microsoft Access, Paradox, FileMaker Pro, or Visual FoxPro, which enables you to sort your contacts based on any field of information and to address envelopes or labels if you want to send out mailings to a large number of contacts. Email applications and other programs on your computer frequently offer an address book component in which you can track your network.

Handheld Devices

Personal Digital Assistant (PDA) devices that you can synchronize with your computer are among emerging tools for networking, and many models of cell phone offer similar capabilities for organizing your contacts. You can use your computer to create contact lists like the one on page 102 and then import your contacts database into your phone or handheld device for easy access. You can also easily

DUCKS IN A ROW

=============={FOOT NOTE}==============

You may also find yourself sending text messages from a handheld device
or cell phone and instant messages from your computer for networking
communications. Writing for Forbes.com, Scott Reeves advises that messages
sent this way must grab the receiver's attention in the first three to five
seconds. Recruiters have told him that messages from job seekers must
convey in the first five lines of the text message the sender's identity, type of
job sought, and what the candidate offers. Text messages are also great
for sharing bits of news with your network contacts.

NAME	CO. NAME	TITLE	PHONE	FAX	E-MAIL	HOME PHONE	ADDRESS	COMMENTS
Deborah Mittman	UniSOAR	Mkting Analyst	803-555-9284	803-555-9074	Mitt1@aol.com	803-555-1045	PO Box 1923, Columbia, SC 28540	Met at a Conference
Keith Cannon	Barnes & Co.	Mkt. Researcher	843-555-8182	843-555-7734	KC55@yahoo.com	843-555-0092	58 Ross St., Charleston, SC 28540	Very helpful
Jon Patrick	ReddiNet	VP Marketing	843-555-8763	843-555-0004	jpvp@red.net	843-555-7654	177 3rd Ave., Myrtle Bch, SC 28539	Gave resume critique
Jason Pauls	Taylor Industries	Mkting Director	214-555-6742	214-555-6744	pauls@taylor.com	214-555-2678	1465 Sycamore Ave., Dallas, TX 75260	Deb Mittman's former supervisor at UniSOAR
Teresa Vincent	Roderick Ent.	Mkting Analyst	843-555-6914	843-555-6825	tvince@aol.com	843-555-9486	466 Cavour St., Charleston, SC 28540	Granted informational interview

send your own contact information to other networkers when you're in a mingling situation. You may have noticed that college-age networkers rarely write down phone numbers anymore; they simply punch them into their cell phones.

Organizational Schemes

No matter how you choose to record your contacts, you may choose to organize them alphabetically, by the date you met them, by the date of last contact, by city or geographical region, by industry or job type, or by degree of importance or helpfulness to you. You may also want to look for commonalities that provide the impetus to introduce members of your network to each other. Many types of indexes are available for both binder and card systems. Consider whether a system of color coding might be helpful to you. You may want to make a record of each communication you have with a member of your network, along with comments about the encounter. That way you can track who is due for a follow-up, and you can ensure that you don't make a pest of yourself by contacting people too often.

=[FOOT NOTE]=

Consider keeping a network journal during your search. In it, you can record all your contacts and networking activities, as well as comments on what worked and what didn't. Next time you need to network, you can use your journal as a guide instead of starting at square one.

PART THREE

NETWORKING

IN THE WORLD OF WEB 2.0

CHAPTER 15

NETWORKING VISIBILITY AND BRANDING

Networking venues have changed and expanded significantly since the first edition of *A Foot in the Door*, and most of that change is driven by technology, especially a growing number of tools on the Internet known collectively as Web 2.0. While Web 2.0 is much more complex than a set of applications and platforms for networking, one succinct definition of Web 2.0 by web guru Tim O'Reilly is that it comprises an "architecture of participation." The concept of Web 2.0 "suggests that everyone . . . can and should use digital media to express and realize themselves," writes Andrew Keen in the *Daily Standard*. In other words, the Internet now offers unprecedented and growing opportunities for people to interact, network, socialize, share information, make themselves known, express their opinions, demonstrate their creativity, and more.

Web 2.0 has enabled job seekers to enhance their visibility in both the online and offline worlds. Visibility would not seem at first glance to relate directly to networking. In the world of Web 2.0, however, the old networking cliché, "It's not what you know but who you know," becomes, "It's not what you know but who knows you." Clearly, you can enhance the effectiveness of your networking efforts if lots of people know who you are and have easy access to communicating with you. Raising your visibility becomes a new type of passive networking with some very active elements. This practice of getting your name out there is a form of personal branding, which creates new avenues for raising your visibility and building your aura as an attractive candidate for hire. Elevating the world's awareness of you creates new opportunities for networking, which is a cooperative relationship. This chapter details how to raise your visibility in the offline realm—with the idea that even visibility generated offline may make its way to the Internet—while chapters 16 and 17 focus on online techniques. Increasing your visibility helps your contacts find out where you are and what you're doing. While some techniques in this chapter are much easier for established job seekers than first-time job hunters, entry-level candidates should keep the approaches in mind and plan to implement them in the future as they build expertise and credibility.

How to Be Visible

Before we get into ways you can pump up your online image, try this exercise: Take about a minute to write down what you are most known for. In what area(s) could you offer yourself as an expert? Ideally, you are considered an expert in some area of your career or professional life, but hobbies and interests can be fair game, too.

And that brings us to the many ways you can get your name out there:

- Be known for your expertise. Offer yourself as an expert to the media. Contact local, regional—and if you're really hot stuff—national newspaper, magazine, and online editors to let them know you'd be willing to be quoted on the topic(s) of your expertise. Your communication with editors could take the form of an email, phone call, letter, or even a "media kit" with business card, resume, and list of story tips for which you're qualified to serve as a source. I recently had a client, for example, who unfortunately did not receive tenure from the university at which he was a professor. He happens to be an expert on terrorism, however, and is often called upon by the media for quotes and insights. His visibility through this media exposure will help raise his currency as he seeks a new job.

- Contact editors and ask if they could use someone to write articles or a column in your area of expertise. The pay may be minimal or nonexistent, but having your name in print and your expertise disseminated can be priceless. Small local weekly newspapers and newsletters are often particularly hungry for this sort of contribution, and trade publications in your field may also welcome a column or article of interest to their readership. This writing effort may not yield a direct networking effect, but it will increase your name recognition and credibility. Ask the editor to run your photo with the column for even more visibility. You'll introduce yourself to someone during a future networking opportunity and hear him say, "Oh, you write that fascinating column in the *Hometown News*."

- Write a branded one- to three-paragraph bio of yourself and include it at the end of every article or column you write (see more about branding on page 113). It can also be used as a basis for an online profile for venues discussed in chapters 16 and 17 as well as information that people can use when introducing you when you speak in public.

- Write letters to the editor of trade publications, business periodicals, and local newspapers.

- Write reviews of books in your area of expertise and submit them to sites like Amazon.com.

- Speak in public. Organizations are always looking for speakers. For most smaller, local organizations, speakers are not paid, but they gain excellent exposure by talking about subjects of interest to the group membership. Almost everyone is an expert in some area, and if your area is related to a career field, you can parlay speaking opportunities into your next terrific job. Know a lot about computers? Good at motivating people? Know how to create an effective web page?

Have your finger on the pulse of emerging trends? The same topic(s) in which you offer your expertise to the media can make fascinating fodder for presentations that will familiarize audiences with your talents and expertise. Your talk will likely be publicized, further enabling you to get your name out there. Oh, and even if it's just rubber chicken, you'll usually get a meal out of your speaking engagements. If you're not comfortable as a public speaker, consider boosting your confidence by joining Toastmasters, which can be a great networking venue in itself. To mine for groups in your area that seek interesting speakers, obtain lists of local organizations from the Internet, library, phone book, chamber of commerce, or newspaper listings of meeting schedules. Call the program chair of, say, a dozen groups, and you'll be amazed how many would love to have you as a speaker—and in the near future to boot. Once you have some speaking engagements lined up, polish your presentation. The more compelling a speaker you are, the better this technique will work. After you've spoken, stick around for the group's social hour. The group's members will be eager to meet you, especially if you've given a fascinating talk. "Automatically, the audience is already interested in the topic simply by being present," observes international trade economist Leroy Smith. "This makes the networking activity much easier." Be sure to bring a healthy supply of business cards. You'll make excellent contacts who will see you as more credible than the average Joe Jobseeker because you've demonstrated your expertise. Jennifer Sumner, an organization development consultant and executive coach for Boeing, scored a networking success when she conducted a personal growth group. "One of the group members encouraged me to talk with the owner of a management consulting firm he used in his business," Sumner remembers. "The firm hired me." Consider, too, that you can convert your oral presentation into an article for publication in the group's newsletter for even more visibility.

- When you're not the speaker, ask questions and make comments during the Q&A period at presentations or meetings. Be sure you introduce yourself so observers will know who's asking the question. This type of visible inquisitiveness paid off for a networker observed by networking expert Debra Feldman. Here's how he told his story of attending a conference at which he talked to a well-respected chief finance officer (CFO) at a company in his industry: "During the conference I asked some relevant questions. At the time, I wondered if my questions would show my lack of knowledge in certain aspects of our business, but I wanted to know so I asked. Six months after that conference, I had been out of work for one week when that CFO tracked me down because he had an opportunity for a new position. He remembered me because of the questions I asked. I am now in that position."

- When you're in a speaking or networking situation, wear something that makes you feel fantastic about yourself. Brand yourself with a distinctive feature of your attire that people will always associate with you—perhaps a pin, scarf, or boutonniere.

- Offer your services to local colleges and universities. Make yourself available as a guest speaker for collegiate groups and clubs. Consider applying as an adjunct instructor. Many schools welcome professionals—even those without terminal degrees—to bring their real-world business experience to the classroom. Let college and community groups know that you're also available for panel discussions and roundtables. Any event that increases your visibility can be a terrific networking opportunity. If you have the resources, you can even produce your own workshops and seminars. Contact local colleges and universities to see if they'd be willing to host your presentations. Many schools have continuing-education and Elderhostel programs that are always looking for good instructors.

- Be visible in professional, volunteer, and civic associations, such as the chamber of commerce and Rotary. Membership in these organizations is a great way to network, but to really get your name out there, run for office and volunteer to serve on committees.

    Serve on advisory boards and boards of directors. At some point in your career, you may be asked to participate on a corporate or nonprofit board, either in a decision-making or advisory capacity. If you're looking for a terrific networking opportunity—as well as visibility—jump at the invitation to join a board. Membership on some boards is by application rather than invitation; check into boards associated with your local government, for example. My county government in Volusia County, Florida, has several dozen advisory boards open to local residents—from the Commission on the Status of Women to the Cultural Arts Advisory Board. Although board membership is a serious responsibility and time commitment (boards generally meet anywhere from quarterly to monthly), it can be a rewarding networking opportunity because of the accompanying clout and prestige. Board membership frequently affords you the chance to rub elbows with some of the most powerful members of the community or corporate world—people you might not normally get to meet. To maximize the opportunity, don't just sit there at meetings and say "yea" or "nay"; get actively involved. Volunteer for committees. The more you do for the board, the more people you'll be able to network with and the better known you'll become.

- Anytime you achieve a major accomplishment or make a career move, send out a press release. Most local newspapers have a regular column in their business section precisely for chronicling the career transitions of people like you. Trade publications also frequently have such columns. Your press release should be brief and to the point, and you can get a good idea of how it should be worded by looking at the blurbs in your chosen publications' columns. The release is usually headed with contact information about you in case the editor has any questions, along with the words "FOR IMMEDIATE RELEASE." The release should be double-spaced. Check with the editor about submission preferences; in this electronic age, most editors prefer that you submit your release in an email message or as an email attachment. You should also submit a nice headshot photo of yourself, also ideally as a digitized file (for example, in .jpg or .gif format). The advantage of this publicity is that it can keep every member of your network informed about what you're up to. As you write regular notes to members of your network, the blurb about your latest move is a perfect piece to clip and send to your contacts, especially those in far-flung locales who may not have seen the item in the publication. Executive recruiters, a.k.a. headhunters, also watch these columns to keep an eye out for promising people they'd like to recruit.

- Enter contests designed to recruit job candidates. An emerging trend in recruiting is to run contests to determine which candidates have the best skills in a given area. For example, the website TopCoder (www.topcoder.com) runs software-programming contests. Many professional organizations also offer contests.

Personal Branding and the Promotional Tools That Grease the Networking Wheels

Increasingly, the most successful job seekers present themselves as a brand. Deborah Wile Dib, a CEO coach, notes that "companies and recruiters are looking for . . . candidates with strong brands—clearly defined value propositions and differentiators. They are looking for fit. They are looking for authenticity and passion—the courage of a candidate to be real. Candidates need to stand out from thousands, even millions, of others."

But how do you stand out? Dib continues, "Recruiters and companies want candidates who are less 'transactional' (translation: task-oriented) and more 'relational' (translation: branded, visible, active, networked). Companies and recruiters want candidates who can clearly and effortlessly articulate a differentiated and powerful value proposition (translation: the most compelling reason they should be hired!)."

While the foregoing visibility techniques can solidify and publicize your brand, don't go anywhere without your resume and business cards, and make sure the text and graphic images on these pieces carry a consistent message. That message comprises your branding. A network contact who looks at your resume should be able to instantly conjure up an image of who you are and the value you offer an employer.

Determine what your brand is and capture it in a concise branding statement, which William Arruda and Kirsten Dixson describe in their book, *Career Distinction: Stand Out by Building Your Brand* (Wiley, 2007), as "the attributes that enable you to deliver value." A first step to determining your brand is to think of three major trends—ongoing patterns of delivering value—that have spanned your career; for example, you've always been a people person. Excellent resources that describe processes for developing a branding statement include Arruda's and Dixson's book, as well as *Brand Yourself: How to Create an Identity for a Brilliant Career* by Andrusia and Haskins (Ballantine, 2000).

- A highly motivated, experienced professional with skills in marketing, e-commerce, relationship building, promotion, and management.

- Positioned to draw on record of achievement and success to deliver exceptional sales results that maximize unequivocal strengths as outstanding, top-producing sales professional.

- Poised to contribute strong interpersonal, communications, and organizational skills and experience to your organization in a front-line, customer-support role.

- Delivering project-management expertise, along with unsurpassed business analysis and application design, development, and implementation proficiencies, to organizations seeking a dynamic, self-motivated professional to build winning partnerships that produce exceptional results.

- Specializing in raising the bar, creating strategy, managing risk, and improving the quality and caliber of operations.

- Delivering entrepreneurial insight and marketing expertise to build winning partnerships and produce exceptional bottom-line rewards.

- High-performing, senior-level, training professional eager to provide leadership and deliver results.

- Delivering cutting-edge business-to-business and business-to-consumer strategic marketing and product-development methodologies that produce highly successful product-positioning initiatives and result in exceptional bottom-line results.

- Dedicated nursing professional committed to excellence in patient care and poised to deliver unsurpassed, individualized nursing care in an acute care setting.

- Delivering leading-edge innovation to IT solutions.

- Poised to deliver operations and human-resources management methodologies in a management role requiring out-of-the-box innovation and creativity to support organizational goals.

- Delivering project-management leadership using state-of-the-art methodologies and collaborative brainstorming strategies that culminate in exceptional operational outcomes.

- Providing executive-level administrative support services through strong interpersonal skills, unsurpassed organizational abilities, face-of-the-department front-line professionalism, and highly successful career experiences.

- Ideally positioned to contribute to your organization exceptional teaching and curriculum-planning skills, based on a career of more than fifteen years of professional cosmetology achievement.

=={FOOT NOTE}==

Whether using the verbal or written tools of networking, you'll make a lasting impression on your contacts if you are passionate about your field and the job you hope to attain.

RESUME

Always keep your resume updated, and always keep fresh copies in a place where you can easily access them. A slim portfolio that you carry with you is best. Your briefcase is also a possibility, although you may not be carrying it everywhere you go. At least keep some copies handy in your car so you can fetch them when the occasion arises. Make sure the copies are clean and crisp, not tattered or dog-eared. Look for paper companies that sell matching letterhead and business card stock. For networking, it's especially important to have as much information as possible on your resume about how to contact you, and be sure to also include your branding statement for a consistent message. Your resume has a twofold purpose when you're networking. You can give it out when people ask for it or when you otherwise sense an opportunity. But you can also ask your contacts for advice about it. Often they will want you to leave it with them so they can take time to digest it and formulate suggestions. The result is that you will have not only obtained a critique but also given your contact a "leave-behind" containing all your information. Whenever you feel it's appropriate, ask your contacts if they'd like extra copies of your resume to distribute to others.

An emerging trend is a one-page networking resume, a pared-down version of your resume that makes for quick reading by your contacts.

[FOOT NOTE]

Don't be afraid to get creative with printed pieces you hand out when you're networking. Consider the impact a colorful brochure or newsletter might have on your contacts. Maintain the same branded look for these pieces as you have initiated for your resume and cards.

BUSINESS CARD

Always keep a plentiful supply of updated business cards with you whenever you network. They are the stock-in-trade of networking. But what if you're currently unemployed or a not-yet-employed college student? Or if you desire to change careers and want to project branding that is different from your current job? In those cases, use a networking card.

NETWORKING CARD

A networking card is exactly like a business card, but for people not currently employed. It contains all the information about how to contact you. Instead of listing your job title and where you work, it lists your area of expertise and what you have to offer. Include your branding statement on your networking cards. Your cards should not only convey the same image as your resume, but should also reflect content consistency; in other words, the pieces should look like a matched set with the same color scheme, fonts, graphics, and general type of paper (although the card will typically be on heavier card stock).

You can order networking cards from a printer or office-supply company or online just as you would order business cards, but it's easy to make networking cards inexpensively on your own. Most office supply stores sell 8½-x-11-inch sheets of business-card stock in various colors and designs (ideally, as mentioned, get card stock that matches your resume). They are designed to be printed on your laser or inkjet printer. To set them up on your computer, use the template function of your word-processing program. When they come out of the printer, you separate the cards at the perforations, and voilà—networking cards. Here's a sample of what a networking card might look like:

WEB PAGE: www.snicker.com/~kacosta/

KATE ACOSTA
Systems Analyst

Product rollout and expansion strategist with heavy
network systems connectivity experience

717-555-1939
EMAIL: kacosta@snicker.com
FAX: 717-555-1861

RESUME HIGHLIGHTS CARD

To take your business or networking card to the next level, you can
have highlights from your resume printed on the back of it. The card
is useful for times when it would be awkward or inappropriate to distribute your resume. Obviously, you can't fit your whole resume on the
back of a card, but you can fit a key word, skills, or qualifications sum-
mary. The resume highlights card might look something like this:

QUALIFICATIONS SUMMARY

Business-partnership development
Corporate image enhancement
Business structure experience
E-commerce expertise

CHAPTER 16

SEARCHABILITY AND
YOUR ONLINE PRESENCE

Have you ever Googled yourself?

You know . . . have you entered your name into the well-known Internet Google search engine to see how many times and in what context your name appears on the Web? To get a fairly accurate reading, place your name in quotation marks in Google, for example, "Katharine Hansen." If you have a very common name, add some other identifying information, such as your middle name, the town you live in, college you attend, email address, or your employer: for example, "Katharine Hansen" "DeLand, Florida" "Quintessential Careers." Once you've done a search, you can set up a search "agent" to alert you anytime anything new appears on the Web containing your name.

What does this little exercise have to do with networking? Even if you've never Googled yourself, it's possible that an employer or recruiter has. It's part of an increasing practice—especially at senior and executive levels—to find out how visible a prospective employee is. The number of citations or "hits" on Google (or other search engine) is considered a reasonable gauge of a candidate's visibility and online presence and tells the employer or recruiter what kind of information is available online about the job seeker.

"If you don't have an identity on the Web, you don't exist," stated Ross Mayfield, CEO of Socialtext, an enterprise social software company, in an article published in NewsFactor Network online publication. A New York resume writer tells the story of submitting names of two executives to a recruiter who was unimpressed with both candidates—one because his name was nowhere to be found on the Web, and the other because the controversial political views he published online turned the recruiter off. Another career expert tells of trying to look up an old colleague and finding only outdated information on him on the Web. Had the colleague ensured that his online information was current and visible, the career guru would have referred him to a great job opportunity.

According to a study by ExecuNet, three out of four recruiters conduct Internet searches on candidates. "Smart hiring managers will always Google their prospective people," says Allison Hemming, president of the Hired Guns, a New York interim-staffing company, in an article on CareerJournal.com. Some career experts, in fact, predict that future job openings won't be advertised at all and that employers will simply find candidates through such means as online searches.

Your Online Presence

So, how do you enhance your online presence and Googlability? A significant way to build an online presence is through the personal branding discussed in chapter 15, which may include your own website with such ancillary components as an online portfolio (including your resume) and a blog—or any of these items as a stand-alone feature. The other major way to enhance your online presence, participating in online networking venues, is discussed in chapter 17.

PERSONAL WEBSITE

A personal website with a portfolio shows employers that you are technically savvy, open to new trends, and poised on the cutting edge. A portfolio published on the Web enables you to include links to all kinds of items that tell more about you and your capabilities and provide evidence of your accomplishments (writing samples, graphic-design samples, ad campaigns, photographs, PowerPoint presentations, reports, graphs, charts, lists of accomplishments and awards, executive summaries, case studies, testimonials, project deliverables, business plans, designs, and even multimedia items such as video and sound clips) that employers can access 24/7. A number of Internet service providers offer free space on the Web; see the Resources section for how to find free web space.

A website, of course, is not a printed item, and you're not about to go around giving out printouts of your web page. Yet, a personal website can be an excellent networking tool. Even if your website contains nothing but your resume, it will go a long way toward enhancing your online presence. When Seattle-based Alice Hanson was recruiting for a large software company, she described how she would find candidates: "The first thing I do is go to Google and look for resumes that are posted to the Internet. These are the first people I call because their resumes are free," she explained (recruiters must pay to access resume databases on sites such as Monster and CareerBuilder).

Let's look at a scenario in which the web page might come into play:

You, on the phone with a prospective network contact: Hello, Mr. Marks, my name is Tom Butler. Peggy Freedman suggested that you would be a great person to talk with about the publishing field. I'm an English teacher considering a move into that field and I wondered if I could have a few moments of your time to talk about it.

Mr. Marks: Sure, that would be fine. It would assist me, though, if I could see your resume. I think I could be more helpful if I knew more about your background. Can you mail or fax me a copy?

You: I think I can get my resume in front of you even faster, Mr. Marks. Is your web browser open?

Mr. Marks: Yes.

You: My resume can be viewed on my web page at www.plex.com/butler_resume.html. The web page also has links to writing samples so you can get a better idea of my abilities.

Mr. Marks: That's great! I'll look it over and give you a call back later this afternoon with some suggestions.

If you have a website, be sure its address appears on all your printed materials, too. Convey a consistent branding message and professional, business-like image throughout your website. You'll often find some elements in a web portfolio that you wouldn't find in a typical resume—photos of the candidate, for example, which facilitate a sort of virtual networking through which employers can get to know prospective employees better. The portfolio provides a great opportunity for the candidate and employer to build rapport before an interview even takes place.

For examples of web portfolios, see mine at www.quintcareers.com/KHansen_Portfolio.html and my partner Dr. Randall Hansen's career portfolio at www.careerdoctor.org/Coaching_Portfolio. Another nice portfolio—Alex Bischoff's at www.handcoding.com/portfolio/—shows the candidate's web-development skills.

BLOG

A web log, popularly known as a blog, can be linked to a personal website or portfolio or can be a stand-alone element for building your

---

={FOOT NOTE}=

Consider purchasing a so-called "vanity domain" for your website, portfolio, or blog. A vanity domain, available for a fairly inexpensive monthly fee, has your name built into it, such as this example from one of my former students, Kyle Luikart: www.kyleluikart.com.

personal brand and online presence. *NetLingo: The Internet Dictionary*, defines a weblog or blog as a "frequent, chronological publication of personal thoughts and Web links. A blog is often a mixture of what is happening in a person's life and what is happening on the Web, a kind of hybrid diary/guide site, although there are as many unique types of blogs as there are people." Like a personal website, a blog can facilitate online networking by enabling people to find you. In addition, these online journals often encourage interactive networking by inviting readers to comment.

Writing for MarketingProfs.com, Debbie Weil says that "if ever there were a perfect tool for the job hunter, blogging is it." Weil advises blogging about a topic you're passionate about, writing short and frequent entries, ensuring correct grammar and no misspellings, organizing your blog well, and including key contact information so employers and recruiters can find you. "Blogologist" Alex Halavais, interviewed by Danielle Sacks for *Fast Company*, suggests blogging with the idea of attracting people in the same profession, as well as reading and commenting on other blogs. See, for example, the blog of Nina Burokas (http://blog.ninaburokas.com), a blog about branding for people interested in this topic.

A blog provides an excellent way to showcase your expertise to a relatively wide audience. Halavais, for example, notes that a "medium" blog readership of one thousand people a day can mean an additional one thousand souls who will have the blogger in mind when a job opens up. "I never would have expected this as a benefit," writes Jason Alba, CEO of JibberJobber.com (www.jibberjobber .com), "but one of the most powerful networking things I've done this year has been through blogging. Whether it's because of my own blog or because of the comments that I've made on other people's blogs, this has been a totally unexpected benefit of blogging."

Beware of Digital Dirt

Keep in mind that employers and recruiters aren't just looking for how many times your name pops up in an online search. They're also interested in how positive your online image is. Thus, you need to be very careful about how you project yourself online. The Internet is a highly public medium, and personal information floating out there in cyberspace about your political affiliation, religious preference, and even your family could unfortunately work against you. There's a fine line between opening enough of a window into your personality to intrigue a prospective employer and turning a visitor away with off-color humor or inappropriate photos showing your partying. Never depict in words or photos illegal or unethical activity. Keep a lid on any content involving sex, drugs, or heavy alcohol use. The advice of an anonymous blog contributor is worth heeding: "Never post anything that you wouldn't be willing to read on the front page of the *New York Times*." (Others have similarly cautioned against any material you wouldn't want your mother to see.) Employers are always looking for ways to screen you out. In the previously mentioned study by ExecuNet, one in four recruiters said they had dropped candidates based on the results of the search.

Keep in mind, too, that digital dirt isn't always under your control. Your friends could post questionable photos of you on other sites or you could be negatively characterized on a site whose content is out of your control. That's why it's a good idea to Google yourself to see what's out there. If you find material out of your control, politely ask the site owner to remove it. Also, be sure that plenty of positive, branded material about you comes up in a search by using the techniques in this chapter and in chapter 15. A plethora of positive material may counteract any negative content.

CHAPTER 17

BUSINESS AND SOCIAL ONLINE NETWORKING

In chapter 16, Alice Hanson revealed that, while recruiting candidates, Google was the first place she looked. "The next," she said, "is for members of professional organizations and people listed in Zoom-Info (a site that provides a compilation of any mention of a person anywhere on the Web in any search engine) and on LinkedIn.com." Research by the Society for Human Resource Management affirms that commonly used techniques for finding candidates include scanning social networking sites and viewing industry-specific blogs and discussion forums. This chapter discusses online networking tools like ZoomInfo and LinkedIn that can help you enhance your network and your visibility to employers.

Online Communities
PN2PN

Online communities are among networking's fastest-growing trends, approaching cult status and representing a phenomenon sometimes called Personal Network to Personal Network, or PN2PN, in which users can build vast networks and tap into them for social, business, and career needs. Users boast of having tens of thousands—even hundreds of thousands—of people in their networks. Research by the Institute for Corporate Productivity, Inc., indicates that 65 percent of business professionals use these communities, of which 35 percent use them for job seeking. Among the more well-known of these networks are LinkedIn and Ryze. Among networks that are far more social than business/professional are Friendster, Xanga, and MySpace. One that began as a network for college students is Facebook, which now endeavors to be a social platform for everyone.

ONLINE DISCUSSION GROUPS

Another major category of online community comprises online discussion groups on every imaginable topic, also known as special-interest groups, forums, or Listserv electronic mail lists (so called because of the Listserv software that operates them). Andrea Dine of Boston's Center for Career Development notes that she belongs to two professionally specific online discussion groups that have been "invaluable networking resources." Similarly, survey respondent Doug Strasnick recalls a friend who landed interviews in his quest for a cable-TV producer job by networking on related message boards. In the past, I've belonged to groups for writers, public information officers, people interested in women's studies, and many others. Web addresses of many online communities can be found in the Resources section. On the off chance that you cannot find online groups to match your interests or situation, it's easy to start your own at sites like Yahoo! Groups (http://groups.yahoo.com) and ezboard (http://ezboard.com). Members generally interact with these discussion groups through email, although many discussion groups are web-based, enabling you to interact with them through your web browser instead of by

========={FOOT NOTE}=========

Among other types of online communities are groups in which alumni from a particular school can network, groups for former employees of specific organizations, sites such as Squidoo that enable individuals to establish themselves as experts on their passions, discussion groups that focus on employment issues, and networking organizations with an online presence.

email. Members of these groups have the opportunity to ask questions, obtain career advice, and access the job postings that may be sent to the group.

PEOPLE FINDERS

Another twist on online networking involves tools such as Ziggs and PeopleSpot, which are designed to find people on the Internet. Let's say you'd like to network with an old friend you've lost contact with. These tools often enable you to track down the missing would-be member of your network and reconnect. A slightly different permutation is Plaxo, a free service that updates and maintains the contact information in your address book.

CHAT ROOMS

Still another category of online networking venue is the chat room. Available on the Web or through such providers as AOL, chat rooms revolve around a wide variety of professional and personal interest areas. The advantage these chat areas have over online discussion groups is that they allow real-time conversation. A message sent to an email address might sit for anywhere from a few minutes to a few days or longer without getting a response, while chat-room input generally gets an instant response. Chat rooms provide good networking opportunities because of the way they simulate actual conversation. Variations on the chat room include instant messaging and ICQ ("I seek you"), other formats that allow conversation in real time. See more about chat rooms in the Resources section.

Advantages of Online Communities

Many respondents to the research survey for this book indicated that, rather than as venues for adding new contacts to your network, the best use of these tools is for maintaining contact with people you already know or finding familiar contacts you've lost touch with; for example, Erica S. Whitfield, a career expert in Virginia Beach, Virginia, says, "Online avenues of networking have helped me reconnect with *so* many people, and I have found it to be highly effective!" Similarly, Laura M. Labovich, president of A & E Consulting, LLC, a northern Virginia–based career coaching and human resources consulting company, said, "I personally have had loads of success using LinkedIn.com, because I've been able to reach out to many old friends and acquaintances from various points in my life and learn about what they are doing and, in turn, they usually know someone who is searching for a job or needs a new resume." Still, many job seekers find new contacts through these venues, including recent grads who locate alumni through sites like Facebook and more established networkers who use sites like LinkedIn to locate employer information and key contacts with high-level executives. These venues, of course, also boost job seekers' visibility and online presence, facilitating their being found by employers and recruiters. One career professional observed that online networking venues can be effective for those too busy to do a lot of face-to-face networking.

Your Online Profile

Given that the linchpin of most online networking venues is the profile that users complete, online networkers should develop their profiles with care, using the same personal-branding concepts as outlined in chapter 15. As Walter Akana, life strategist with Threshold Consulting, Incorporated, noted, "A lot of people don't leverage their online networking memberships with effective profiles that reflect a personal brand." Ensure that your profile is not only branded, but also interesting, engaging, intriguing, and rich with industry-specific keywords. "The more you share about yourself, the easier it will be to make connections," advises Shally Steckerl, who has written extensively about social networking sites. Similarly, the more valuable information and expertise you contribute to these venues, the more you will enhance your reputation.

One respondent pointed to the effectiveness of finding people through their profiles on Ryze and then meeting them through networking events that Ryze allows members to publicize on its site: "Ryze has provided the platform for other members and me to meet and even continue communicating online, but the deciding factor for many of the projects is meeting face-to-face and feeling comfortable working with the other person."

Online Risks

Do remember that these online networking activities are often time-consuming—and can keep you glued to your computer instead of getting out there and making face-to-face contacts. Mix up your networking efforts to include an online component, but don't network online to the exclusion of real contact with live bodies.

Whether you join an online community and post a profile or contribute to online discussion groups, watch what you say. Speaking your mind, especially among those connected with your professional field, certainly adds to your online authority, but don't forget the very public nature of the Internet and the possibility that a prospective employer could read what you say. A comment that you innocently post to an online discussion group could be viewed negatively. Sites frequently cited as especially subject to risky postings were those that appeal primarily to younger people, such as MySpace and Facebook. Alan Finder of the *New York Times* reports that "college career counselors and other experts say some recruiters are looking up applicants on social networking sites like Facebook, MySpace,

══════════════[FOOT NOTE]══════════════

Several sites, such as LinkedIn and Yahoo! offer sections that give members the opportunity to post and answer questions. Both asking and answering questions can raise your networking visibility.

Xanga, and Friendster, where college students often post risqué or teasing photographs and provocative comments about drinking, recreational drug use, and sexual exploits in what some mistakenly believe is relative privacy." A case in point was a flap over Miss New Jersey 2007 against whom a blackmailer threatened to go public (unless she relinquished her crown) with embarrassing photos from a page on Facebook. The beauty queen had designated the page as private, which means that only invited friends are allowed access to it. Even with such protections, as Miss New Jersey learned, virtually anything on the Internet can become public and thus seen by prospective employers. If you are averse to removing the racy side of you from your profile on a site that's heavily slanted toward social networking (Facebook, MySpace), set your profile to private so only those in your friends network can see it—as long as you realize that even that precaution may not keep background checkers at bay. You can also try to avoid using your real or full name on these sites. Tools such as ClaimID (http://claimid.com) are also available to help you manage your online identity. (See more about digital dirt on page 124).

A university career-services staffer who responded to this book's survey cited another risk of online networking—a client who thought he was building a network with a manager in a chat room found that the person he was chatting with was someone completely different. Similarly, a career professional surveyed for this book reported on a young woman she knows who was terminated during a probationary period from her job with a well-known company after someone found her profile on MySpace and saw some racy photos taken at a party, along with some unsavory comments about how uptight her boss was.

The bottom line on online social/business networking? The Internet-based forms of networking described here are well worth exploring. My research indicates, however, that networkers are only beginning to use these tools, effectiveness is unproven, and success stories are limited. (Note that the Internet offers lots of material on how to make the most of the best-known social/business networking tools.) In addition, many sites, motivated by profit, change their rules and protocols periodically. The savvy networker is wise to question how much time should be invested in online networking. Younger job seekers, for whom MySpace and Facebook have become a way of life, will likely adapt well to devoting a significant chunk of their job-hunting time on networking sites. Still, for any job seeker, face-to-face relationships are the gold standard and yield the richest results, so online venues should be used judiciously as tools that generate person-to-person meetings and close connections.

PART FOUR

INFORMATIONAL INTERVIEWING:
THE ULTIMATE NETWORKING TECHNIQUE

CHAPTER 18

WHAT IS
INFORMATIONAL INTERVIEWING?

One out of every two hundred resumes (some studies put the number as high as fifteen hundred resumes) results in a job offer. One out of every twelve informational interviews, however, results in a job offer. That's why informational interviewing is the ultimate networking technique, especially considering that the purpose of informational interviewing is to gather information, not solicit job offers. Job offers just happen to be a delightful side benefit of this valuable practice.

Informational interviewing is just what it sounds like—interviewing designed to produce information. What kind of information? The information you need to choose or refine a career path, learn how to break in, and find out if you have what it takes to succeed. Informational interviewing is an expanded form of chatting with your network contacts. It's the process of engaging one of your network contacts in a highly focused conversation that provides you with key information you need to launch or boost your career. The term *informational interviewing* was invented by Richard Nelson Bolles, author of the best-selling career guide of all time, *What Color Is Your Parachute?* (Ten Speed Press, updated annually). Bolles refers to the process as "trying on jobs to see if they fit you." He notes that most people screen jobs and companies after they've already taken a job, while informational interviewing gives you the opportunity to conduct the screening process before going after or accepting a position.

An informational interview is not the same as a job interview by any means, but it is probably the most effective form of networking there is. I require my students to perform three informational interviews per semester. Most of them are skeptical about the assignment in the beginning, but I can't tell you how many have ended the semester amazed and delighted with how much they learned and how influential the process was for their careers. I'm not the only teacher whose students have been thrilled with informational interviews. Terry Carles, a student recruitment counselor at Valencia Community College reports, "I teach career development, and my students are required to do an informational interview. Every semester someone returns with a job or internship from their experience. One student completed an informational interview with a network administrator, and returned the next week with a . . . job offer."

I've had students who have realized that, as a result of informational interviewing, their career paths and even their majors were totally wrong for them. They made this discovery when there was still time to make a course correction. Others haven't needed such a drastic change but have adjusted their assumptions and expectations based on what they learned in the interviews. When you are

========={FOOT NOTE}=========

Although informational interviewing is well known and highly promoted in the world of career counselors, it is an underused—and often even unfamiliar—practice among job seekers. My students have repeatedly demonstrated the value of informational interviewing, especially as a self-discovery tool. As one student wrote, "The informational interview process was extremely eye-opening. I went from a clueless college student to a directed job seeker. Before this experience, I was unaware of how helpful talking with professionals can be. I was able to ascertain what these jobs really entailed. I got a feel for what the working world is all about. My conversations with my interviewers gave me a window into how to get into the job I want. I learned from people who are living my dream now that I need to prepare for the future."

considering entering or changing to a certain career, it just makes all kinds of sense to talk to people in that field. Yet most people never do. They trust their professors, textbooks, or romantic notions about professions gleaned from TV or movies. When you really think about it, you miss out on an incredible opportunity if you fail to research your career field by talking to people in it.

The Best Way to Learn What You Really Want in a Career

Because of the exploratory nature of informational interviews, they are particularly effective for those, such as college students, who are just embarking on their careers. They are also an excellent tool for career changers who want to find out what's involved in the career they are considering entering. Even for those who don't wish to change careers but do want to change jobs, informational interviews can be a helpful way of discovering what working for other companies would be like. A job seeker who conducts an informational interview usually has his career path illuminated in one or more of the following ways:

- The inexperienced job seeker learns about the realities of the work world and what to expect.

=====[FOOT NOTE]=====

My students have found that informational interviewing arms them with the wisdom to make better decisions, as this student describes: "Informational interviews gave me an opportunity to explore the knowledge, advice, and experience of successful professionals. They helped educate me about current employment conditions, the future of the field, and the many other aspects essential in choosing a career direction. Following the interviews, I found I was better equipped to make decisions about my future and definitely more comfortable in making those decisions."

- The job seeker learns what types of opportunities are available in a given field, including jobs and career paths she may not have known existed.

- The job seeker's career aspiration is affirmed. The dream career turns out to be everything he thought it would be.

- The job seeker's career path is reinforced, but she learns that more training or more polished skills will be necessary for success in the field. Or the job seeker learns of her professional strengths and weaknesses and often receives a resume critique. The job seeker sometimes has an opportunity to promote her strengths in a nonthreatening environment.

- The career the job seeker always wanted turns out to be wrong for him. I had a student who began the semester 100 percent sure he wanted to be a stockbroker. After interviewing three stockbrokers, he ended the semester 100 percent sure he did not want to be a stockbroker. Similarly, a career expert in Syracuse, New York, learned through informational interviewing that he didn't want to be a reporter, technical writer, or efficiency expert. Many job seekers learn through informational interviews that the career's average salary, working conditions, or opportunities for advancement are not what they imagined. Or they learn that the career just doesn't fit their personality.

- The job seeker who interviews people in several different careers obtains the information needed to choose among various career paths. Or the job seeker who is set on a general path to pursue narrows down a specific niche through informational interviewing. A new graduate who wants to get into marketing, for example, may decide as the result of informational interviews whether to pursue marketing research, sales, or promotions.

- The job seeker who conducts informational interviews with several companies discovers an excellent fit within an organization and decides that it would be a wonderful company to work for.

- The job seeker gleans the information needed to develop a strategy for entering her career of choice.

- The job seeker clarifies values, realizing what's really important in life and choosing a career that allows him to embrace what's important.

You Can Benefit from Informational Interviewing at Virtually Any Stage of Your Career

- The early stage, when you are exploring which career path to pursue

- The middle stage, when you are finalizing career choices and deciding on a niche within your career path

- The late stage, when you are deciding which companies to apply to and preparing to interview for jobs

=={[FOOT NOTE]}==

Informational interviewing makes the work world real to those who haven't yet experienced it, as one of my students noted: "It wasn't until I conducted informational interviews that I began to assess my career objectives for the first time—thinking about the environment I would like to work in, the types of people I want to work with, and the schedule I would have.

It is because of the interviews that my career objectives have changed somewhat, and I have come to realize exactly what I would like to receive and give back to my future job."

- The stages revisited, when you are ready to change careers and begin the cycle anew

- The stage in which you don't want to change careers, but you'd like to explore other companies to see if the grass is really greener

Several survey respondents for this book cited success stories for clients other than the college-age job seeker who typically conducts informational interviews. Terri Ferrara, a Career FIT and Job Search Expert in Traverse City, Michigan, with Summit View Career Coaching, cited one of her clients, an established job seeker who received and accepted a job offer at an informational interview. "She still loves her job after a year," Ferrara said. Sandra Lim of A Better Impression told the story of a successful informational interview in her own career. She had interviewed for a job for which she was the number two candidate and was not hired. A year later, a professional colleague who worked in the same company Lim had targeted agreed to an informational interview. "It turned out by this time the successful candidate had left for another company, and I was offered the job I originally applied for!" Lim reported.

A Way to Tap into the Hidden Job Market

Informational interviewing is one of the best ways to mine the hidden job market because of the depth and quality of information the practice provides. Those who conduct informational interviews can learn

- The needs of the company or department that is the subject of the interview. Armed with this knowledge, the job seeker can later approach the company with a description of how she can meet these needs (see part 5).

- Valuable insider knowledge about how to break into and succeed in the chosen career and company. Consider a future job interview in which your competition is someone who has conducted an informational interview with a company employee and you haven't. Who do you think will have the edge in the job interview?

- The names of other companies that may be hiring.

- The names of other contacts who can become part of the job seeker's network.

- Timely information about industry trends and issues, which can provide an inside edge in the job search.

- How to "speak the language"—the jargon of the industry.

- Unadvertised job openings within the company. Sometimes the unadvertised opening is the very one your informational interviewee is leaving! Tammy Bowen, a director of career planning, tells of conducting an informational interview when she was relocating to a new area. The woman she interviewed had just accepted another position elsewhere and called Bowen to ask if she would be interested in taking her job. Bowen was then invited for a job interview and was subsequently offered the job, which she accepted. The same thing happened to Jerry Falco, director of the Career Development Center at Lycoming College. "I got my first job after college in a matter of days through networking," Falco recalls. "My girlfriend's sister was dating a pharmaceutical salesman. I called [him] for an informational interview. The salesman gave me the district manager's name and number. The salesman had just announced his plan to continue his education full-time, and a replacement was needed. I did not know this when I called. I called the district manager and arranged a meeting for the next morning. I was offered the job less than a week later."

Informational Interviewing to Build Networking Relationships

At the very least, you can count each informational interviewee as a valuable member of your network of contacts. Because your conversation with an informational interviewee will tend to go into greater depth than your chats with other members of your network, you will generally forge a stronger and more memorable bond. Informational interviewing builds relationships with people who become invested in your career, will remember you, and will be eager to hear about your progress. As a survey respondent points out, contacts made through informational interviews can even become valuable mentors.

People in the world of work are generally delighted to give informational interviews for the same reasons they are willing to be included as a member of your network. They like to talk about themselves and give advice. They are often especially eager to do their part to recruit a new member of their profession and encourage those just starting out in the field. Information and advice are easy to give, as opposed to actually trying to place people into jobs.

Practice That You Can Apply to Job Interviews

An informational interview is not the same as a job interview. Essentially, you are in control of an informational interview; you set the agenda, you ask the questions. Despite the differences, however,

=========================[FOOT NOTE]=========================

Informational interviewing is a great way to get your networking feet wet, as one of my students learned: "The informational interview experience taught me a lot about myself, the importance of communication skills, future contacts, and how the interview process works. Throughout the interview process, I wasn't certain about my future direction, but as the interview process evolved, so did I."

informational interviewing gives you valuable practice in talking with people one-on-one in a professional setting. Because the atmosphere of the informational interview is relatively relaxed compared to that of a job interview, you can use these situations to bolster your confidence so you are exuding self-assurance when you interview for an actual job opening. The more informational interviews you conduct, the more confident you will be. My students have also discovered that informational interviewing helps them practice their communication skills, their listening skills, and their ability to interact with many types of people. Wrote one of my students, a senior finance major: "Informational interviewing has helped me realize how important communication skills are in pursuing success. Before the interviews, I was never a person who would approach someone much older than me and strike up a conversation. After conducting the interviews, though, I have much more confidence in myself and know that if I wanted to have a conversation with someone more experienced than me, I could."

What It's Not: A Sneaky Way to Interview for a Job

The practice of informational interviewing is not without its abusers. Too many job seekers have arranged interviews on the pretext that they are informational but then have tried to turn the sessions into job interviews. So much abuse has occurred, in fact, that some employers are extremely wary of being interviewed, while others have been burned and refuse to be fooled again. If you've had any thoughts of trying to be dishonest about your motives for informational interviewing, put this book down and hang your head in shame. Ask yourself if you would hire someone who had deceived you about the purpose of his interview with you. And trust me when I tell you that informational interviewing is phenomenally effective without any deceit. Job and internship offers often result from informational interviews, but getting offers should not be the purpose of the interviews. Remember that the information and insight you gain from this process is exceedingly valuable in its own right.

INFORMATIONAL INTERVIEWING GIVES HER
THE CONFIDENCE TO CHANGE HER LIFE

"I did not want to do informational interviews because I am rather shy. I knew that it would be so hard for me to call up people and ask them questions. I actually feared it. I turned to my parents to ask for their help. Luckily, they had a multitude of friends and business associates I could interview. My first interviewee quickly started to change my mind [about informational interviewing]. This interviewee obtained her job through an informational interview. When I learned this fact, I started to take notice of how beneficial these interviews could be if I used them. I found myself having shorter versions of informational interviews with a variety of people. At work, I would ask the district manager how he started out or, when the vice president came to the store, I would ask him a few questions. I realized that if I had never done the interviews, I would have been too scared and insecure to go over and talk to someone I did not know.

"Finally, I was starting to realize what informational interviews were about and how I could use them in my career. I began to think about all the people I had talked to, and I began to look at my future very differently. I always thought that I would finish college, go on to law school, graduate, and get a job as a lawyer for a big corporation. I had never questioned that path. I thought it was the only logical way. This misconception was changed after these interviews. I began to think that there were so many different things I could do, things I had never even imagined. I spent a great deal of time thinking about the variety of careers in a different light. I was not distinguishing them by how much they paid or the status I would receive from them anymore. I was now looking at all the different aspects about them. I began considering the number of hours I would have to work, if I would have to relocate, and if it would allow me to obtain my other goals as well.

"The informational interviews taught me one other lesson that has had the biggest impact on my future—all the options I had. It is an amazing experience the first time you realize you're no longer a child and you are actually going to enter the real world soon. I am not inexperienced; I supported myself through college by working full-time as a waitress. I always thought I would wait tables till I graduated from law school. I remember the day my opinion changed, and so did my future. I was no longer happy with my job; I was miserable. One day I sat there listening to the manager of my restaurant complain about things going wrong, all of which were obviously her fault. I began to ask her a couple of questions, the same questions that I had asked my informational interviewees. I discovered that this woman had not been to college, held no degree, and had been promoted on a fluke. I sat there thinking that this woman is in way over her head and she has no idea about what it takes to run this restaurant. I thought of all the simple lessons and ideas I had learned in school and how they could reform this restaurant immediately.

"That was it! I could do this. I could manage a restaurant. I had finally realized that I had a great education and four years of experience working for me. I spoke to my parents and really believed that I was going to let them in on this big secret. I was wrong. I was met with a response that shocked me, 'Of course you can do it.'

"All of a sudden I looked at myself differently. I was not only an adult, I was an adult with an education that has given me a field of choices. So I did it. I grabbed the newspaper and began looking for jobs. I found [an ad for] one and decided to give it a try. I rewrote my resume and sent it out. Four days later I received a call from a company to set up an interview. I was on my way. I have begun to plan my life differently, investigating what I could do with the degrees I have now—not waiting until law school is over.

"These informational interviews taught me so many things. I now realize I have so many wonderful things I can do with my life, not three years from now, but now. I never thought I would say I was happy to do informational interviews, but now I can say that this one activity changed my life for the better."

CHAPTER 19

HOW TO FIND AND CHOOSE INTERVIEWEES: NETWORK, NETWORK, NETWORK

The easiest way to find prospective informational interviewees is through networking. Anyone in your network can either be the subject of an informational interview or suggest others to interview. The ideal subject of an informational interview is someone who is in a job you'd like to have, either in the near future or someday. The interviewees in higher-level jobs you'd like to hold someday can be advantageous because they may also possess hiring power. Naturally, if you interview someone with hiring power, you increase your chances of receiving a job offer as a direct result of the informational interview. But remember that obtaining offers is not the purpose of these interviews. It's fine to interview people with hiring power, but you will likely learn more from people at your own level (and, depending on your level, your peers may have hiring power anyway). Favor information over influence, but aim for a mix of interviewees with and without hiring power.

Even if you are still unsure of what you want to do in your career, you may find that informational interviews are helpful in narrowing down your list of career choices. Chances are that you are considering a few careers at the top of your list—choose the top three and line up interviews with people in those fields. This process of interviewing may help you decide what path you want to follow.

Scrutinize your network for people who would make good informational interview subjects. Among the best sources for informational interviews for college students and new grads are alumni, especially recent alumni who are in the kind of job you expect to occupy right out of college. Company representatives who recruit on your campus are also good targets for informational interviews. They are frequently asked to perform this function, and they are also usually quite adept in providing information on working for their company.

The best sources for informational interviews for established job seekers and career changers include members of professional organizations. If no one in your network fits that description, start asking members of your network to suggest people who hold the type of job you'd like.

Don't be afraid to shoot for pie-in-the-sky interviewees. If you'd love to interview Steve Jobs, Oprah Winfrey, or Bill Gates, but, not surprisingly, no one in your network knows one of these superstars, try approaching them cold. Granted, success is pretty unlikely, but it can't hurt to ask, and some powerful titans of business have actually granted informational interviews on occasion.

David Helfand, coordinator of career counseling at Northeastern Illinois University, tells of working with a graduating college senior who had played on the college baseball team and was a marketing major seeking a position in sports marketing. He requested informational interviews with all the major sport teams in his home city of Chicago and ended up with an internship with the Chicago White Sox.

Once you've identified some people to interview, you can approach them using the suggestions in chapter 20.

How many interviews should you conduct? As a matter of fact, informational interviewing can be a rich and fulfilling lifelong process. You could spend your whole career learning about other people's jobs while enjoying your own. You can also spend a lot of time on informational interviewing in the early formative years of your career when you're still exploring what you'd like to do. It's wise to interview several people in any one type of job to get a variety of perspectives. You wouldn't want to base your whole opinion about a given job on an interview with someone who was burned out on the position or carrying a chip on his shoulder.

The number of interviews you conduct at any given time when you are searching for a job will depend a great deal on the urgency of your job hunt. On one hand, informational interviews are time consuming, both to arrange and conduct. On the other hand, they are highly effective. If your job search is urgent, employ other networking techniques and conventional job-search methods, but always keep at least a few informational interviews in the mix. While I assign my students, generally college juniors, to do three informational interviews as part of my class, I would probably assign at least ten, if I could. You will be your own best judge of how many will benefit you and your career.

CHAPTER 20

HOW TO SET UP INFORMATIONAL INTERVIEWS

Before you even approach your prospective interviewees, you need to think about what you are actually requesting.

Deciding on a Framework: in Person, by Phone, or via Email?

Should you ask to conduct the interview over the phone, through email, or in person? Face-to-face interviews are by far the most valuable and effective. To talk to someone in her own workplace environment can be so much more instructive than talking over the phone or online. You can observe the corporate culture during an in-person interview. You are also more likely to make a lasting and productive connection with your interviewee and receive a job offer.

=====================[FOOT NOTE]=====================

As with any networking, making that first contact can feel like a major obstacle, especially if you're shy. Once you do it, as one of my students learned, it gets a lot easier: "I learned quite a bit about myself while doing these interviews. Some of my biggest faults have shown up . . . including overwhelming shyness. I had to learn to be assertive . . . to call up complete strangers and ask for interviews. I became more outspoken and confident."

Face-to-face interviews are not always possible, however. Sometimes geography is the obstacle; someone you'd really like to interview is just too far away to make a visit practical. Time constraints also may play a role. Even though a phone or email interview can be just as time consuming as a face-to-face meeting, prospective interviewees sometimes perceive in-person interviews as more of a disruption than those conducted via other means.

Ultimately, the framework should be the interviewee's decision, but when you initially approach the subject to request an interview, it's a good idea to express your preference.

How Much Time Should You Ask For?

The rule of thumb for informational interviews is to ask for twenty to thirty minutes. Once you're in the interview, it's important to stick to that limit unless you get clear signals from the interviewee that he would like the meeting to continue.

Using Referrals to Help Set Up Informational Interviews

People in your network can be invaluable to you in setting up informational interviews. They can help in two ways.

They can directly run interference for you by contacting someone you'd like to interview. Let's say your Uncle Ed knows the head honcho at a company you'd love to work for. Uncle Ed calls Mr. Big and, after the appropriate small talk, says, "My nephew, Charlie, is looking for a job in your field and would love to conduct an informational interview with you to find out more about your career. Do you mind if he contacts you to arrange an appointment?" Mr. Big responds, "No problem. I'd love to help out. I look forward to hearing from Charlie."

Members of your network can also assist you by simply allowing you to use their names as a referral. In that case, perhaps Uncle Ed hasn't gone so far as to pave the way for you but says it's fine to use his name. Thus, when you contact Mr. Big, you can say, "My uncle, Ed Matthews, suggested I contact you to see if you might be able to meet with me for thirty minutes to tell me about your career."

What to Include in Your Request for an Interview

Whether you initially write, call, or email, your request should:

- Identify you

- Explain why you're contacting this person

- Tell how you got the person's name, if applicable

- Assure the prospective interviewee that you need only a brief meeting

- Assure her that you are not looking for a job in this interview (if these concerns arise)

- Offer in-person, phone, or email choices for conducting the interview

- Express appreciation to the prospective interviewee for considering the interview

Writing Letters or Sending Emails to Request Informational Interviews

Unless you are extremely adept at using the phone and rejection rolls right off your back, you will probably find it much easier to write a letter or send an email message first, and then follow up with a phone call. The following sample letters are easily adaptable as email requests. Be sure to keep copies of all your correspondence.

A FOOT IN THE DOOR

LETTER FROM A COLLEGE STUDENT

Dear Dr. Buddinger:

As a junior at Franklin and Marshall College, I have begun taking classes in my major field of psychology. I am especially interested in the pediatric therapy track, and I would like the opportunity to schedule an informational interview with you to learn more about the day-to-day activities of a pediatric therapist.

I was fascinated with the approach to pediatric therapy that you described in your recent article in *Pediatric Therapy Today*, and I am convinced that you would be one of the most enlightening people in the field that I could possibly interview.

I know you are very busy, so I assure you our meeting will be brief. It would be wonderful for me to meet with you face-to-face and see your clinic, but I am also open to interviewing by phone or email. I'd like to give you a call next week to schedule about a half hour of your time, at your convenience.

Thank you so much for considering this request.

Cordially,

Pippa Carson

LETTER FROM A CAREER CHANGER BASED ON A REFERRAL

Dear Mr. Skaarsgard:

I am a high school art teacher seriously contemplating a career change to the art conservation field. Regina Twigg told me about your wonderful gallery and suggested that you could offer a unique perspective on this career field.

I would appreciate the opportunity to meet with you and discuss your work and the trends in the field. I am especially interested in your views regarding conservation and restoration of Native American artwork. Any insights you have would be greatly appreciated.

I do not intend to take more than about thirty minutes of your time. I would be pleased to meet you in person and view your gallery; however, I would also be willing to interview you by phone or email.

I will contact your office the week of September 17 to see if we can set up a mutually convenient time for this informational meeting.

Thank you very much for your consideration.

Sincerely,

Ted Thistlebine

LETTER BASED ON PREVIOUS ENCOUNTER

Dear Ms. Milton:

I really enjoyed meeting you after your presentation at the last meeting of the Brandon County Human Resources Association. Your talk was truly inspiring.

I am currently a personnel generalist looking to expand my horizons within the human resources field and would welcome the opportunity to hear more of your insights into the profession. Your position sounds very much like the type of work I'd like to do.

Would you have time in the next few weeks to meet with me for about a half hour? I'd like to ask you a few questions about your role in this profession. I would be happy to come to your office to talk, but if it would be more convenient, we could conduct the interview by phone or by email.

Thank you so much for considering this request. I'll contact you next week to see if we can schedule time to meet.

Cordially,

Pamela Hotchkiss

CAREER CHANGER'S COLD-CONTACT LETTER

Dear Mr. Pondo:

As an aspiring management consultant, I have been impressed with what I've learned about Davie and Associates. Your company's reputation for high-quality work has inspired me to request a brief informational interview with you. I was especially interested to read in the *Wall Street Journal* about your company's new twist on total quality management.

I am completing graduate work in management consulting at Bowdoin College after leaving active military service. I would very much like to talk with you about your work.

Because of the obvious geographical obstacles, an in-person meeting is not practical, so I'd like to interview you by phone or email.

I'll contact you the week of November 19 to see if we can set up a time for a phone or email discussion. I will ensure that the interview does not take more than thirty minutes of your valuable time.

Thanks so much for considering this request.

Cordially,

Dan Deerfield

Phoning to Request an Informational Interview

Your initial request can be by telephone if you are comfortable with speaking to people on the phone. Or perhaps you are on a tight time frame and don't have time to introduce yourself by letter or email. Although it is possible to set up an entire informational interview via email, you will almost definitely have to call your interviewee sooner or later if you've written or emailed first. Never expect the interviewee to contact you.

If your initial contact is by phone, it's extremely helpful to have been referred to your prospective interviewee by a mutual acquaintance. It's also helpful if you're a student, since working people often especially enjoy helping students. Whatever your situation, your call will most likely be intercepted by a gatekeeper—a receptionist, secretary, or assistant. These people need not be thought of as obstacles, and a little courtesy and respect should enable you to connect with the person you want to interview. Let's look at a possible scenario:

Secretary answering interviewee's phone: Bill Jones's office; Nancy Fredericks speaking.

You: Good morning, Nancy (or Ms. Fredericks). How are you today? My name is _____. May I speak to Mr. Jones?

Nancy: Will he know what this is in reference to?

You, if you've written a letter first: I'm following up on a letter I sent him last week.

OR (a bit more boldly): He's expecting my call. (If you said in your letter that you would call, this statement is perfectly true.)

OR (if you've been referred to Mr. Jones by someone else): Stu Ross suggested I call Mr. Jones.

OR (if you're a student): I'm a student at _____ [name of university], and I wanted to see if I could schedule a very brief meeting with Mr. Jones to find out more about his career.

Any of those responses on your part should get you past the gatekeeper. Experts suggest that, in business, Tuesdays, Wednesdays, and Thursdays are less busy than Mondays or Fridays and you will be more likely to be put through on those days. Project confidence, as though you expect to be put through. Often the gatekeeper will be willing to put you through, but it's impossible to do so because your prospective interviewee is out of the office, in a meeting, or on another line. If you are asked if you'd like to leave a message, it's best to inquire about a good time to call back. Since you want to avoid leaving the interviewee with any obligation to call you back, it's better to try to phone him again later. If you've tried repeatedly to call back and never find the interviewee in, you could leave a message asking that he call back, but don't hold your breath.

Many experts advise that if you've tried unsuccessfully a number of times to reach your target, it's okay to employ some techniques for avoiding the gatekeeper altogether. Leaving a voice mail message is more effective than leaving a message with a gatekeeper who is not getting you through the gate. The kinds of people you want to interview often come to work early and stay late. Try calling early in the morning, and you may find your interviewee answering her own phone. Or you may be connected to the interviewee's voice mail. If so, however, remember that the voice mail is just another avenue for paving the way. You don't want to leave the impression that you expect the interviewee to call *you* back. Always keep the ball in your own court. A pave-the-way voice mail message might be:

Hello, Mr. Jones. This is Kitty Farr calling. I am exploring possible career directions and am interested in interviewing you very briefly about your career. I'll call you back on Wednesday morning to talk to you personally about scheduling a short meeting.

SAMPLE PHONE SCRIPTS FOR DIRECT DIALOGUE WITH INTERVIEWEE

Once you are talking with the actual person you want to interview, here are some suggested scripts. Of course, you don't want to sound as though you're reading from a script, but these samples will give you an idea of what to say. Always ask if it is a good time to talk. If the prospective interviewee indicates that you haven't called at a good time, ask if there is a better time to call back.

For a cold call:

Hi, my name is _____. Do you have a few moments? [Wait for a response.] I'm in the process of making some career decisions and have discovered through my research that your company is doing some exciting things. I would like to see if I could schedule an appointment to conduct a short interview with you about your career. I would not take any more than thirty minutes of your time.

For a referral:

Hi, my name is _____. Karen Levy suggested I contact you. Have I caught you at a good time? [Wait for response.] Karen tells me you'd be a great person to talk to about a career in _____. I'm exploring that field and wondered if we might be able to have a short meeting so I could ask you some questions about your career and get your perspective on the field.

For a self-referral based on hearing the prospective interviewee speak:

Hi, my name is _____. I was at the meeting of the American Marketing Association last week and really enjoyed the talk you gave. Do you have a few minutes? [Wait for a response.] I'm interested in breaking into marketing and would love to schedule a brief meeting to get your advice. When I heard you speak, I knew it would be enlightening to talk with you about your marketing career. I need only about thirty minutes of your time.

For a self-referral based on a previous encounter:

Hi, this is _____. I really enjoyed meeting you at Zach Howell's party last Saturday. Our brief chat affirmed my interest in investment banking. Are you terribly busy right now? [Wait for response.] It was great to chat with you, and I wondered if you might have a half hour in which we could continue our conversation sometime soon.

For a student:

Hi, my name is _____. I'm a student at Kensington University majoring in _____, and I'm plotting out my career path. Is this a good time for you? [Wait for response.] Would it be possible for me to conduct a short interview with you so I can get your advice and find out more about your job? I promise I wouldn't take more than half an hour of your time.

For a letter or email follow-up:

Hi, my name is_____. I wrote you a letter last week. Is this a good time to talk? [Wait for response.] As you recall, I am interested in the _____ field, and I wrote to ask if you could spare thirty minutes to talk with me about your career. Do you think we could schedule a meeting?

For a voice mail follow-up:

Hi, my name is _____. I left you a voice mail message yesterday. Did I catch you at a good time? [Wait for response.] As you recall, I was calling to see if I could arrange to interview you briefly about your career.

As the prospective interviewee agrees and begins to suggest times, don't put roadblocks in the way. Do whatever you must do to accommodate the interviewee's schedule. The interviewee is doing you a big favor, so it's your responsibility to be flexible.

Asking in Person for an Informational Interview

There's always the possibility you'll meet someone face-to-face who would make a fabulous informational interview subject. If it's a chance meeting, you might spontaneously mention that you'd love to interview the person. You will probably still have to follow up by phone or email to arrange the actual appointment.

Handling Resistance to Informational Interviews

As noted earlier, informational interviews have been abused to the degree that some employers are wary or downright opposed to them. If a prospective interviewee seems hesitant about your request, don't push too hard. If you sense a crack in his resistance, you can simply assure the person that you seek only information; you are not trying to sneak your way into a job interview. If you are a student, be sure to mention your student status since many employers are more willing to assist students than other job seekers. But if the prospective interviewee seems too uncomfortable with the idea, cut your losses and move on to the next person.

Another type of resistance can come from the prospective interviewee who suggests that you should be talking to the company personnel director or human resources manager. In that case, tell the would-be interviewee that you are not seeking the interview to actively pursue a job; instead, at this stage, you are merely seeking information that will help you make some career decisions.

You might also be told the company has no openings. Again, explain that you are not pursuing openings but simply information; you will not be in a position to seek job openings until you have gathered more information about the field.

Some people might ostensibly be willing to be interviewed but tell you they are too busy. Don't press them, but do ask if they anticipate a time when they might have a few minutes for an interview. Or ask if they know someone else in a similar position who might have time to meet with you—which is also a terrific way to expand your network.

CHAPTER 21

HOW TO PREPARE
FOR AN INFORMATIONAL INTERVIEW

For an informational interview to be truly effective, you can't just go into it blindly. You need to prepare.

Research the Company

Thorough company research is an absolute necessity when you go on a regular job interview. You don't have to do quite as much research for an informational interview, but some degree of research will enhance the quality of the interview. If you are informed about the company, you'll be able to ask more intelligent and relevant questions. You'll respond thoughtfully to information and questions the interviewee might put to you. You won't waste the person's time by asking questions that could have been answered by doing your homework. A wealth of valuable resources are available for company research, many of them right at your fingertips on the Internet. An excellent umbrella website that walks you through the whole process of company research is the Quintessential Careers Researching Companies site at www.quintcareers.com/researching_companies.html. Other resources include:

- **Library reference material.** Check with your reference librarian on how to find company information. Some standard reference sources, both about the companies and occupations in general, include *The Occupational Outlook Handbook*, *The Dictionary of Occupational Titles*, *U.S. Industrial Outlook*, and *The 100 Best Companies to Work for in America*.

- **Library online and CD-ROM databases.** Examples include Lexis/Nexis, ABI/INFORM, EbscoHost Business, NewsBank InfoWeb, Reference USA Business, and Business and Industry News. These databases direct you to articles about companies found in recent periodicals. The database will either direct you to the periodical that contains the article or will actually contain the article in full-text form, accessible right from the database.

- **Annual reports.** You can request them from the company itself. A selection of annual reports may be available in your library. Many annual reports can also be viewed on the World Wide Web. More than one thousand can be accessed through www.reportgallery.com. You can order annual reports through the *Public Register*'s free annual report service at www.prars.com. Many companies also have annual reports for current and recent past years in the investor relations section of their websites.

- **Other company literature.** Contact the company to ask for any brochures, newsletters, or other publications that would familiarize you with the organization.

- **Company web pages.** If you don't know a company's web address, you can try two easy steps. Try typing in www. company name.com, where "companyname" is the actual name of the firm. Or conduct a search on one or more of the Web's many search engines, such as Yahoo! or Google. Another option, of course, is to call the company and ask for the website address.

- **University career services offices.** These offices contain lots of company information for college students, and generally alumni may use the resources of their university's career center as well.

It's also a good idea whenever possible to find out as much as you can about the person you'll be interviewing. If you were referred to your interviewee by someone, ask that person to tell you about the individual you'll be interviewing.

Decide Whether and How You Will Record Information

Consider whether you'd like to document any of what you learn during the interview and, if so, how. You may find it especially helpful to have a record of the interviews if you do a lot of them and want to keep track of which interview yielded which information. Notes can be a valuable resource when, as you switch into full job-hunting mode, you go back and contact the companies you especially liked. When you encounter an employer you'd really like to work for, take notes about the company's needs so you can later use your ability to meet these needs as a selling point when applying for a job there (see chapter 27). You'll also definitely want to jot down the names of any additional contacts your interviewees refer you to. Options for recording information include

- **Taking notes on a small notepad.** Try to be unobtrusive, and avoid writing furiously every moment of the interview. You want to give your interviewee your full attention, so jot down only the most important information.

- **Tape recording.** The most important thing about tape recording is to obtain your interviewee's permission before you record. Use a tape recorder that is small and easy to use so it won't disrupt the interview. With the right software and microphone, a laptop computer or MP3 player (such as an iPod) can be used to record the interview. Also realize that transcribing a taped interview is a time-consuming process.

- **Trusting your memory.** Going into the interview without any way to record what you learn is an option, but you may want to plant a notepad in your purse or car, so you can quickly write down everything you remember right afterward. You will, of course, need to have some way to take down the names and numbers of any referrals you receive.

Plan to Dress for Success

For maximum effectiveness, dress in professional attire for an informational interview—the same way you would for a job interview. Men should wear a full suit with tie; women should ideally wear a skirted suit or very professional pantsuit. Your clothing should be clean and pressed with no rips or tears, and your shoes shined. Wear conservative jewelry and go easy on the fragrance. Be sure hair and fingernails are nicely groomed. Hair should be worn off your face. The interview is a chance to make a positive impression. Not everyone who is gathering information will go to such lengths to look professional. You will distinguish yourself if you look as though you fit in with the organization. Obviously, none of this advice applies to telephone or email interviews, but even when you use those communication channels, you'll project yourself more confidently if you wear something nicer than, say, your ratty old bathrobe.

Update and Bring Your Resume

Let us once again stress that the informational interview is not a job interview. Still, make sure your resume is updated and bring a copy with you. For one thing, your interviewee may well ask for a copy. "After spending ten years in human resources, I'd have to say that if I were meeting with someone for an informational interview and he did not have a resume, I'd think that he was unprepared and therefore maybe not such a top candidate for a future opening," cautions Robbin Beauchamp, employer relations coordinator at Stonehill College. "Job seekers, regardless of age or experience, should be able to easily get their hands on their most current, updated resume. Keep them in the car!"

If you are not asked for your resume, consider asking the interviewee to take a look at your resume at the end of the interview. Ask whether she could offer any suggestions for making the resume a more effective tool for obtaining a job in her field or company. Keep in mind that a request for a quick resume critique will be met much more receptively if you've established excellent rapport with the interviewee. The ability to leave your resume or ask for a resume critique is one clear advantage of conducting face-to-face interviews.

Since some employers like to prepare as much as possible for the interview, you may be asked to send your resume before the interview. Even if you're not asked to, it may be a good idea. After your initial phone or email conversation with the interviewee, decide whether he would benefit from or respond well to receiving your resume beforehand and, if so, send it on.

If you receive advice during the interview for better tailoring your resume to that industry, consider asking—again, only if your rapport with the interviewee has been exceptional—if you can send the resume to the interviewee after making changes and call him for an opinion on the new version.

Having said all this, however, you may occasionally encounter advice telling you not to take your resume to an informational interview. One reasonable justification is that only after the informational interview will you be able to tailor your resume specifically to the kind of job you learned about. "I recommend not taking a resume to an informational interview," says Elaine Balych of Mount Royal College in Canada. "All the information learned in the informational interview is fodder for tailoring your resume to reflect the needs of that employer. If that employer gets your old resume—without the information learned—the job hunter is not positioning herself strategically. What I recommend is that the job hunter be prepared to deal with the request in a very fast turnaround, such as 'I do not have one with me at this time but would be happy to put one in your hands in the next twenty-four or forty-eight hours.'"

Practice with a Friend or Family Member

If you haven't done much interviewing, ease yourself in by interviewing close friends or family members before you conduct an informational interview with someone you don't know well. There's probably a lot you don't know about the jobs of those close to you, so, in addition to obtaining valuable practice, you may even learn something.

Call to Confirm Your Appointment

The day before your interview, call to confirm that the meeting is still on. Confirm also the interview time, and make sure you know how to get to the interview site.

Prepare a List of Questions

Sometimes in informational interviews you'll find that conversation flows very naturally and spontaneously. In most cases, however, you will need to steer the interview in the direction most helpful to you by asking questions. For a thirty-minute interview, a list of fifteen questions should be plenty, but you should be prepared with a few extras in case your interviewee gives very concise responses or wants you to stay longer. The list of one hundred questions in the next chapter would probably be enough to last for days, so how do you narrow down the list? Most important is to ask the questions you most want answered. And you are certainly not limited to the questions in this book.

Keep yes-or-no questions to a minimum. Open-ended questions are far more effective because the interviewee will have to elaborate on the answers instead of responding in monosyllables.

Finally, prioritize your questions: If you don't have enough time to ask them all, at least you will have asked the ones that are most important to you. Focus on questions whose answers cannot easily be found elsewhere, such as in the company literature.

[FOOT NOTE]

Most books on job interviewing suggest questions you can ask an employer during a job interview. Many of these questions can be adapted as informational interview questions. One such book is *101 Dynamite Questions to Ask at Your Job Interview* by Richard Fein (Impact Publications, 2000).

CHAPTER 22

WHAT TO ASK:
100 GREAT QUESTIONS TO CHOOSE FROM

For even more interview questions, go to www.quintcareers.com/ informational_interview_questions.html.

General Questions about Your Interviewee's Career Field

1. What are the various jobs available in this field?

2. What types of training do companies offer those who enter this field?

3. How is the economy affecting this industry?

4. What are the growth areas of this field?

5. What parts of the country offer the best opportunities in this field?

6. What is the typical entry-level salary in this field?

7. What are the salary ranges for higher levels in this occupation?

8. Aside from such visible compensation as money, fringe benefits, travel, and so on, what kinds of mental dividends (such as job satisfaction) does this career yield?

9. What skills or personal characteristics do you feel contribute most to success in this industry?

10. What entry-level jobs offer the best opportunities for learning?

11. What trends in the field would be most likely to affect someone just entering this career now?

12. What is the most important thing that someone planning to enter this career should know?

All about Your Interviewee's Job

13. What was your title when you first started here?

14. What precisely do you do? What are the duties/functions/responsibilities of your job?

15. What is a typical day like?

16. Do you have to put in much overtime or work on weekends?

17. Are the time demands of your job specific to this company, or would anyone in this career be expected to put in the same hours?

18. Do you ever bring work home with you?

19. What kinds of problems do you deal with?

20. What do you do if you can't solve a problem on your own?

21. Do you have to deal with a significant amount of conflict in this job?

22. What systems are in place for dealing with conflict?

23. What constraints, such as time and funding, make your job more difficult?

24. What kinds of decisions do you make?

25. Describe some of the toughest situations you've faced in this job.

26. How does your use of time vary? Are there busy and slow times or is the work activity fairly constant?

27. Which other departments, functional units, or levels of the hierarchy do you regularly interact with?

28. Are there aspects of your job that are repetitious?

29. Is multitasking a skill that is required for this job?

30. What particular skills or talents are most essential to be effective in your job?

31. What are the educational requirements for this job?

32. What other types of credentials or licenses are required?

33. Is graduate school recommended? An MBA?

34. What social obligations go along with a job in this field?

35. What organizations are you expected to join?

36. How has your job affected your lifestyle?

37. What are the major frustrations of this job?

38. If you could change anything about your job, what would it be?

39. Is there a great deal of turnover in this job?

40. What is the job title of your department head or supervisor?

41. If you ever left your job, what would be most likely to drive you away?

About Preparing for This Career

42. Does your work relate to any experiences or studies you had in college?

43. How well did your college experience prepare you for this job?

44. What courses have proved to be the most valuable to you in your work?

45. What courses do you wish you had taken that would have better prepared you?

46. How important are grades or GPA for obtaining a job in this field?

About Your Interviewee's Career Path

47. In what way did this type of work interest you and how did you get started?

48. How did you get your job?

49. Which aspects of your background have been the most helpful?

50. What other jobs can you get with the same background?

51. What is the job above your current job?

52. Where do you see yourself in five years?

53. If you could do things all over again, would you choose the same path for yourself? Why? What would you change?

About the Culture of Your Interviewee's Company or Organization

54. Why did you decide to work for this company?

55. How does your company differ from its competitors?

56. What is the company's relationship with its customers?

57. How optimistic are you about the company's future and your future with the company?

58. Has the company made any recent changes to improve its business practices and profitability?

59. What does the company do to contribute to its employees' professional development?

60. How does the company make use of technology for internal communication and outside marketing (email, Internet, intranets, World Wide Web, videoconference, and so on)?

61. How would you describe the atmosphere at the company? Is it fairly formal or more casual and informal?

62. What are your coworkers like?

63. How would you describe the morale of people who work here?

64. Do you participate in many social activities with your coworkers?

65. Is there a basic philosophy of the company or organization? What is it? (Is it a people-, service-, or product-oriented business?)

66. What is the company's mission statement?

67. Is there flexibility in work hours, vacation schedule, place of residence, telecommuting, and so on?

68. What's the dress code here? Is it conservative or casual? Does the company have dress-down or casual days?

69. What kind of training program does the company offer? Is it highly structured or more informal?

70. Does the company encourage or pay for employees to pursue graduate degrees? Is there a tuition-reimbursement program?

71. How does the company evaluate your job performance?

72. Does the company observe any rituals, traditions, or ceremonies?

About the Company's Needs

73. In what areas do you perceive there to be personnel gaps in this company? If the company had unlimited resources for creating new positions, in what areas do you think those positions should be created?

74. In what areas do you see the company expanding? Do you foresee the opening of new markets or greater globalization? Do you predict development of new products and services? Building of new facilities?

75. What obstacles do you see getting in the way of the company's profitability or growth?

76. If you needed someone to assist you in your job, what tasks would you assign to your assistant?

About Opportunities for Advancement within This Company or Field

77. What is the highest-level job one can hold in this career?

78. What is a typical career path in this field or organization?

79. What is the average time an employee might stay in the job you hold?

80. What incentives or disincentives are there for staying in the same job?

81. Would someone in this field need to relocate to advance in her career?

Seeking Advice If You Are a Career Changer

82. My current career is _____. How easy or difficult do you think it might be to make a transition from that field to your field?

83. The skills I use the most in my current career are
_____. To what extent and in what ways do you
think those skills are transferable to your field?

84. What's the best way for me to get more experience in your
field without taking major steps backward from the level
I've progressed to in my current career?

85. The things I like the best about my current career are
_____. Will I find some of those things if I switch
to your field?

86. The things I dislike the most about my current career are
_____. Will I encounter any of those same challenges in your field?

87. Knowing what you know about your career field, and knowing what I would have to do to get into this field, do you
think you would make the change if you were in my position? If not, can you suggest any other fields that might be
more appropriate for me?

Seeking General Advice and Referrals from Your Interviewee

88. What is the best way to obtain a position that will get me
started in this occupation?

89. What do you wish you'd known before you entered this
field?

90. What are the major qualifications for success in this
occupation?

91. What are the most important skills for a position in this
field?

92. With the information you have about my education, skills, and experience, what other fields or jobs would you suggest I research before I make a final decision?

93. Do you know other people I might contact who have jobs similar to yours?

94. Which professional journals and publications should I be reading to learn about this career?

95. Which professional organizations associated with this career should I join?

96. What kinds of experience, paid or unpaid, would you encourage for anybody pursuing a career in this field?

97. What should I do to prepare myself for emerging trends and changes in this field?

98. If I wanted to obtain a job here, who would be the best person to contact?

99. Would you be willing to answer more questions, by phone or in person, if I need additional advice in the future?

100. [If you feel comfortable and it seems appropriate:] Would you mind taking a look at my resume to see if you have any suggestions?

[FOOT NOTE]

Some questions *shouldn't* be asked in an informational interview:

- Don't ask blunt questions about the interviewee's actual salary.

- Don't ask for a job or ask the interviewee's help in getting you a job.

- Don't ask highly personal questions.

CHAPTER 23

HOW TO MAXIMIZE
THE INTERVIEW EXPERIENCE

Arriving at the Interview

Be sure to arrive on time for your interview. To be on the safe side, plan to arrive ten minutes early and be sure to take your cell phone. If on the way to the interview you encounter a situation (flat tire, traffic backup, detour) that you realize will make you late for the interview, call to tell the interviewee you are running late. Ask if he would prefer to reschedule.

When you arrive, if you are greeted by a receptionist or other assistant, treat that person warmly. Such gatekeepers can be wonderful allies, and you can often learn as much from them as from your interviewees. Take your lead from the receptionist, and if small talk seems appropriate, by all means participate in the chat.

Meeting Your Interviewee

When you finally encounter your interviewee, greet her with a moderately firm handshake and a warm, enthusiastic smile. Thank your

===========================[FOOT NOTE]===========================

To use informational interviews to expand your network, take a list of companies you think you would like to work for. If you have enough time and good rapport with your interviewee, show him the list and ask who he knows at those companies.

interviewee for taking the time to meet with you. In the interviewee's office, wait for an invitation to sit down before making yourself comfortable. Your conversation will probably begin with some ice-breaking chitchat. Make the most of that small talk to set yourself and your interviewee at ease.

Absorbing Your Surroundings

Take in the environment at the company. How does it compare with your expectations? What would it be like to work for this organization? How quiet or noisy is it? What other establishments are nearby? Are there places to go for lunch? What's the parking situation? What's the office setup? Is it "cubicle city," or are there private offices? Do workers have windows and, if so, what kind of view do they see when they look out? Does the office seem pristine and new or shabby and dilapidated? How are people dressed? Are workers interacting, or do they keep to themselves? Does one gender predominate? Do the people seem as though they like their work, or does the atmosphere seem tense? Would you enjoy working there?

Unless your objective in the interview is to find out about the company because you are considering working there, don't be unduly influenced by the physical surroundings. If you are more interested in exploring the interviewee's job or industry than the company, realize that just because one person in this job works in an unattractive environment doesn't mean everyone with that job does. Conversely, don't conclude that a particular type of job is glamorous based on your observations of one person's workplace.

Listening and Observing Keenly

Before you begin your questioning, make a brief opening statement reminding the interviewee of your objective: "I am in the process of trying to narrow down some career choices, and I am interested in finding out more about what your job (or field or company) is really like. I appreciate your taking this time with me." You may also want to share a bit about your background and aspirations. Many interviewees want to know about you so they can tailor their responses to your needs; that's why some ask to see your resume even before the interview.

As you begin asking questions, be sure to listen attentively and enthusiastically to the interviewee's responses. Look for clues to your interviewee's personality and that of his company. When appropriate, use those clues to steer the conversation toward mutual interests. Does the interviewee have lots of photos of his kids around the office? Does the interviewee display any sort of collection (for example, elephant figurines, toy soldiers, or teapots)? Is there interesting artwork in the office? Are there plants or fresh-cut flowers? Is there paraphernalia suggesting an interest in a sport? Does the interviewee's office show him to be a fan of a particular sports team? Feel free to comment about any of these clues. The interviewee will be flattered that you noticed his interests and will probably enjoy talking about them. If the interests are mutual, you can forge an even stronger bond with your interviewee. Just remember that you've asked for only a short period of the interviewee's time, so don't get bogged down talking about your mutual interest in skydiving.

While you should stick relatively close to your scripted questions, don't just become a question-spewing robot. Be businesslike and show that you take the interview seriously, but let some of your personality shine through. Discussing mutual interests is one way, but also be open to spontaneity in the conversation. If something your interviewee says makes you think of a question that's not on your list, don't hesitate to ask it. Be sure the interviewee knows how interested you are in learning about her career and how much you appreciate her information and advice. The interviewee may even start asking you questions; be sure to respond with a bright and energetic attitude. Also look for opportunities to demonstrate that you've done your homework and learned something about the company.

Enthusiasm Is Everything

Employers rank candidates' lack of enthusiasm in interviews as their biggest pet peeve. Interview enthusiasm is key in getting a job. The same principle applies to informational interviewing. If you are enthusiastic about learning about your interviewee, you will make a far more favorable impression than someone who just seems to be going through the motions. Be animated and bubbly, and the interviewee will begin thinking of you as a job candidate even though that's not why you're there.

Knowing When to End It

Keep an eye on the time, but be careful not to keep looking at your watch as though you're bored. As your allotted time draws to a close, make a remark such as, "I don't want to go over the thirty minutes I asked for, so let me ask you one final question." Or "Well, I promised I would only take thirty minutes of your time, so we can wrap up the interview now if you'd like." The interviewee will either accept your invitation to stop or will indicate that he is enjoying the conversation and would like to continue.

=={[FOOT NOTE]}==

To get an even more in-depth feel for what a job or company is like, ask your interviewee if it would be possible to "shadow" her for a half or full day. Don't expect to shadow your interviewee right after your interview, but if you hit it off with her, try to arrange to come back another day and observe as she conducts a typical day's work.

- Asking for referrals. Be sure to ask for names of other people who could give you similar information about the field and be part of your network. Once you are given names, confirm that it's okay with your interviewee for you to use her name when you contact the referrals. If you feel you have especially good rapport with the interviewee, you might ask if she would be willing to pave the way—by contacting the referral and telling him to expect to hear from you.

- Asking for the interviewee's business card and if you can stay in contact.

- Thanking the interviewee. (You'll do so again in writing; see part 5.)

[FOOT NOTE]

What should you do if you are really offered a job or internship? If you're truly in an exploratory phase and are not yet sure of your career goals, you may want to wait until you've conducted more interviews before jumping at an offer. But if the timing and the job are clearly right for you, by all means take the offer (perhaps after thinking about it and discussing it with appropriate members of your network).

HOW TO TRACK AND ANALYZE
YOUR INFORMATIONAL INTERVIEWS

Particularly if you conduct a large number of informational interviews, you may want to develop some sort of record-keeping system. You may very well consider your informational interviewees to be members of your network and track them the same way you track other network contacts (see chapter 14). But you may want to keep some sort of journal or notebook to record and analyze information and impressions collected in the interviews. This information will prove extremely valuable when you later approach the interviewee or company again in search of a job instead of information, and it will enable you to demonstrate inside knowledge of each company and its needs.

You could organize your records by interviewee, or by type of job, or by company, recording key facts and personal reactions. If your main goal is to include your informational interviewees as members of your network, then organize by interviewee. If your goal is to explore careers and try to decide which path to follow, organize by job type. If your goal is to choose which companies you'd most like to apply to, organize by company. On pages 181–83 are samples of forms you could use to record information for each of these three organizational schemes. You can adapt these forms to your own needs, type them up on a word-processing program, print them out, three-hole-punch them, and place them in a binder.

Try to evaluate your informational interviews objectively. Don't automatically decide that you don't like a certain job just because you didn't have good chemistry with one of your interviewees or found the workplace drab. Consider the big picture. As you assess your experience from each interview, ask yourself some of the following questions:

- Could I have done anything to improve each individual interview?

- What did I learn about myself?

- What did I learn about the things I value in a job and in a workplace?

- How does each job align with my own interests, abilities, and goals?

- What were the positives and negatives of each interviewee's job?

- What did I learn about how to break into my preferred field?

- What did I learn about how to succeed in my preferred field?

- How do my skills/grades/experiences/personal characteristics measure up to what's required for entry or success in my preferred field?

- Do I need more training or experience to get where I want to be in my preferred field?

- Assuming I still want to pursue my original career direction, what is my strategy for seeking a job in this field?

- If I have decided against my original field, what fields am I now considering, and how will I find out if another field suits me better?

- What further information do I still need to obtain?

- What should I do next?

INFORMATIONAL INTERVIEW
[RECORD BY INTERVIEWEE]

Name of interviewee:

_____

Interviewee's job title:

_____

Company name:

_____

Company address:

_____

Office phone:

_____

Fax:

_____

Email:

_____

Other contact info
*(home address, home phone,
cell phone, and so on):*

Highlights of conversation:

_____

Advice given by interviewee:

_____

Interviewee's interests
*(based on observations and/or
conversation):*

_____

Referrals provided by interviewee:

_____

Other companies interviewee
suggested exploring:

_____

Resume suggestions from interviewee:

INFORMATIONAL INTERVIEW

[RECORD BY JOB TYPE]

Type/title of job:

_____

Interviewee(s) holding this job:

_____

Observations about workplace:

_____

Typical duties/functions/
responsibilities of job:

_____

Typical day:

_____

Types of problems:

_____

Pace of job
(for example, always hectic, generally
slow, a combination):

_____

Degree of supervision
(Is job highly supervised or are workers
in this job relatively self-directed?):

Level of excitement
(Do interviewees find it exciting or
boring?):

_____

Skills needed:

_____

Education and preparation needed:

_____

Outside obligations, expected
organization membership:

_____

Level of job in relation to rest of
company:

_____

Next level above this job:

_____

Opportunities for advancement:

_____

Recommended route to break into this
type of job:

INFORMATIONAL INTERVIEW

[RECORD BY COMPANY]

Name of company:

Interviewee(s) working at this company:

Contact information for this company *(names of key hiring managers, addresses, phone numbers, fax numbers, cell phones, email addresses, website):*

Reputation of company:

Key products/services:

Company size:

Stability:

Growth potential:

Expansion plans (new markets/products/services):

Company organization:

Types of positions at my level:

Working conditions:

Characterization of people who work here:

Training program(s):

Encouragement or reimbursement for advanced degree:

Professional development opportunities:

Advancement opportunities:

Possibility of relocation:

Salary structure:

Fringe benefits and perks:

Observations of physical surroundings:

PART FIVE

NEXT STEPS:

USING NETWORKING AND INFORMATIONAL INTERVIEWING AS THE LAUNCH PAD FOR YOUR JOB SEARCH

CHAPTER 25

THE FINE ART OF FOLLOWING UP WITH NETWORKING CONTACTS

Very few actions in the world of networking are as important as thanking those who have helped you in your job search. Anyone who provides even the minutest amount of assistance should receive a thank-you. That simple gesture of common courtesy and thoughtfulness will do more to endear you to members of your network and cement your bond with them than anything else. Because they will think of you as a conscientious and gracious person, they will be more likely to recommend you for jobs.

You can get even more mileage out of your thank-you and follow-up efforts with some extra touches:

- Send your contacts clippings of articles of interest to them with a sticky note attached that says, "Saw this article and thought of you."
- If your company produces publications that would be of interest to your contacts, have them placed on the subscription list.
- Consider sending amusing cartoons you've clipped or even photos.
- Send a quick postcard to mention how much you enjoyed meeting a new contact. A picture postcard of a local site can make an inexpensive yet memorable impression.
- Make the saga of your job search fascinating reading as you update your contacts. Describe amusing anecdotes and interesting or famous people you may have met while networking.
- For someone who has been helpful beyond your wildest dreams, a grand gesture, such as sending flowers or taking her to lunch, would not be out of line.
- Send holiday and birthday cards.

Conversely, your failure to thank people will do more to damage your efforts than anything else. George Moskoff, managing partner at the consulting firm Adderly Page Group, reports having spent considerable amounts of time meeting with colleagues, asking them questions, and offering advice. "Rarely do I get a note thanking me for my time," he writes in *Manage* magazine. "It hurts."

Corresponding with your network contacts keeps your name in front of them, so they may think of you when an opportunity comes up that would be a good fit for you. Sending thank-you and follow-up letters also keeps members of your network informed of your progress. Tell those who've given you advice about the results of your following the advice. Moskoff notes that letting members of your network in on the process of your job hunt can be even more important than making contact initially. He suggests letting your contacts know "what you're doing, whom you're interviewing with, how the interviews went."

A thank-you to your network contacts can be in the form of a handwritten social note or greeting card. It can also be a typed business letter. You can send thank-yous by email for immediacy, although it's a nice idea to follow those up with a "hard copy" note sent through the mail. At the end of your job search, when you've found a wonderful new job, send a thank-you to everyone who helped in any way. Following are some sample thank-you notes:

Thank You for Help Provided by a Network Contact

Dear Jackie:

I'm writing to thank you for agreeing to be a member of my personal network. This is an important time in my life as I take the plunge to change careers, and I truly value the advice of professionals like you who know the physical therapy field so well.

I especially appreciate your offer to coach me in interviewing for a job in this field. As an insider, you can provide interviewing tips that few others can.

Jackie, thanks again for your willingness to help me launch this next phase of my career. Don't hesitate to let me know if you think of any additional suggestions or names of people I should contact.

Sincerely,

[Name]

Update on Progress

Dear Mr. Byron:

I just wanted to drop a line to thank you for your continued support and to keep you abreast of recent progress in my job search.

I've had half a dozen promising interviews in the past few weeks. No offers yet—but three of the firms have invited me back for second interviews, so I'm very excited!

I would never have come this far without your encouragement, Mr. Byron. You will be among the first to hear the news when I land my dream job!

Best regards,

[Name]

Follow-up on Advice

Dear Ms. Allyson:

I just had to write to let you know that your suggestion to join my local chapter of Women in Engineering really paid off! Thank you so much!

I went to my first meeting earlier this week and met some wonderful women. I even landed an interview with Bernadette Donaldson. I will be sure to let you know how it goes.

Joining this group was a great suggestion, and I wouldn't have thought of it on my own. I certainly welcome any additional suggestions you might have or names of people who might become part of my network. Please also keep me in mind if you learn of anyone in the industry who could use someone with my skills and experience.

Yours,

[Name]

Sharing Information

Dear Dr. Dorchester:

I just wanted to touch base with you and say hello. My job search continues to be productive, thanks in large part to your many suggestions.

I've just learned that Dr. Joseph Reedy will be speaking in town next month. I know you have followed his theories closely, so I wanted to make sure you were aware of his upcoming lecture. I've enclosed an article on Dr. Reedy, which includes details about the lecture.

Thank you again, Dr. Dorchester, for all your support. I hope I see you at the lecture.

Sincerely,

[Name]

Thank You for Informational Interview

Dear Mrs. Mays:

I can't thank you enough for taking time out of your busy schedule so I could conduct an informational interview with you. I learned a great deal from my time with you.

While many aspects of the hydrogeology field are quite different from what I previously thought, I am more excited than ever about the profession.

Mrs. Mays, you were extremely generous with both your time and information. You have contributed immeasurably to my career development, and I thank you very much. I especially appreciate your suggestions for tuning up my resume. I'm also glad you invited me to keep in touch and apprise you of my career progress, because I fully intend to do so!

Cordially,

[Name]

Thank You at End of Job Search

Dear Sam,

I wanted you to be among the first to know that my job search has ended! After a lengthy search and several months of interviews, I accepted a position with Polymers Unlimited, an international corporation headquartered in Columbia, South Carolina. Even though the company is quite large, the marketing department is made up of just three of us.

I really have a lot of fun there. I am responsible for all of the marketing communications. I love it. I know I am going to learn so much; the firm is great about arranging additional training for employees. The company will be sending me to newsletter seminars, software classes, you name it. I believe I have really found what I love to do.

You were so instrumental in my search, and I can never thank you enough. You gave me invaluable ideas and advice and so many referrals. I am very grateful.

I have enclosed a business card for my new position. Please keep in touch, and if there's ever anything I can do for you, don't hesitate to call on me!

Yours,

[Name]

⟮FOOT NOTE⟯

At the end of your job search, throw a big party and invite your whole network. What better way to thank everyone—and your party might just provide networking opportunities for others.

CHAPTER 26

HOW TO USE NAME-DROPPING REFERRAL COVER LETTERS

Anytime a member of your network gives you the name of someone who might be able to offer you a job, you have the opportunity to write what I have dubbed the "referral cover letter." A referral cover letter, accompanied by your resume, is more likely to result in an interview than almost any other kind of cover letter. Why? Because when you drop the name of someone both you and the recipient of the letter know, you get the recipient's attention. Further, the recipient is more inclined to interview you to avoid seeming rude to your mutual acquaintance. That's just one reason networking is so valuable; the more people there are in your network, the more opportunities you will have to write this extremely effective type of cover letter.

Another type of referral cover letter is the self-referral, in which the person who has "referred" you to the letter's recipient is none other than yourself. The recipient is someone you've met in some context, such as in an informational interview, social situation, or professional meeting. It could also be someone you haven't met but

---

====={FOOT NOTE}=====

To learn more about how to write a cover letter, see my previous books, *Dynamic Cover Letters: How to Sell Yourself to an Employer by Writing a Letter That Will Get Your Resume Read, Get You an Interview, and Get You the Job* and *Dynamic Cover Letters for New Graduates* (both published by Ten Speed Press, 2001, 1998).

---

have corresponded with or talked to over the phone. You use the self-referral cover letter to remind the recipient of your acquaintance. Following are some samples:

College Student Referral Letter

Dear Ms. Timothy:

Your colleague, Jack Waycross, suggested I contact you about the possibility of a full-time position with SpringSweet. As a senior student earning a Bachelor of Business Administration degree from the University of Minnesota, I am ready to make a meaningful contribution to the SpringSweet marketing and sales team.

Both my academic career and employment experience have prepared me well for a career with SpringSweet. My challenging and competitive academic program has included such unique courses as consumer behavior, channels and physical distribution, leadership seminars, and production and operation management. In addition to my schooling, I have worked in the marketing department of Daisy Products, where I added to my sales and marketing experience.

My previous employers can verify that I am an enthusiastic and effective salesman. During my summers at Daisy, I consistently maintained the highest seasonal sales totals. In addition to my previous job experiences, my position as a member of the Minnesota men's soccer team has provided me with significant leadership skills, as well as the ability to work well with a team.

Because you undoubtedly know that a letter and resume can convey only a limited sense of a person's qualifications, I am convinced that it would be productive for us to meet in person so I may present my credentials more completely. I will contact you in a few days to arrange a meeting. Should you wish to reach me before that, my number is 555-1927. Please feel free to leave a message if I am not available. I am looking forward to meeting with you.

Thank you for your time and consideration.

Sincerely,

Max Bonwit

Established Job Seeker Referral Letter

Dear Mr. Sabovsky,

John Winterrowd and I have been talking about how my skills might fit in at InfoSource. He said he'd discussed with you the possibility that I might assist you in your customer service department, so I wanted to introduce myself and tell you a little of what I've done since working with John at GalleryPlex.

I have extensive customer service experience in the high-energy _____ field and I plan to make customer service my life's work. My abilities to communicate effectively, handle customer problems quickly and personably, and work well in high-stress situations have helped me to succeed in every position I have held.

In addition, I have excellent organizational and writing skills, as my former employers can attest. I am currently training to enhance my computer skills, and I have the desire and competence to learn quickly.

I know you won't regret giving me an opportunity to show you what I can do. I am very interested in working for your company, and I believe that you will be happy with my performance.

I will call you in a few days to arrange a time when we can meet in person.

Sincerely,
Maggie Seaborn

Self-Referral Letter Based on a Social Encounter

Dear Mr. Jackson,

As you may recall, we met at Louise Baptiste's Memorial Day barbecue. I came away from our stimulating conversation about trends in the media thinking that I would love to work with you. When Louise suggested that I apply for the available position in your public relations department, I was thrilled with the idea. It would be wonderful to work for your prestigious company, and I am ready to join your outstanding team.

I know that you need someone who is enthusiastic and task oriented, and I am uniquely qualified for the job. Some people are great team performers, while others are better working on their own—I am both!

My success in setting up media features and interviews for San Diego State Bank and the bank's stellar reputation in the media show that I am a top-notch publicist. My position as the mayor's public information officer gave me the chance to organize events and handle media requests in a high-pressure environment.

I am fluent in Spanish, which, as you know, is imperative to your industry in Southern California. I also have excellent computer skills, as I work daily with the Microsoft Office programs and the Internet.

As you can see, I am a dynamic person with a passionate interest in your company. My background has provided me with the skills to be an asset to you. My outgoing personality, accompanied by my profit- and task-oriented work style, makes me an excellent choice for the job.

I will contact your secretary this week for an interview. I look forward to speaking with you again. Thank you for your time and consideration; I hope to see you soon.

Sincerely,

Sally Ringo

Referral Letter Based on an Informational Interview

Dear Mr. Newcom:

Last October I conducted an enlightening informational interview with Krista Tillikum, your human resources associate director. She suggested I contact you when the time came for me to actively seek a human resources position.

I am a highly motivated, hard-working person with a track record to prove it. I have recently graduated from Fairleigh-Dickinson with a degree in business administration and I am eager to put my education to work in a job such as the human resources generalist position you have open.

In addition to my education, I have a five-year history of steady advancement with the university libraries, where I participated in the interviewing, hiring, and training of more than one hundred individuals. I am looking forward to proving myself in the field of human resources, where I hope to find a satisfying and productive career.

From my work experience, I know the value of a good employee. Previous employers will affirm that they have entrusted me with major responsibility and that I adapt well to change. I have a strong work ethic and I am confident that I will be an asset to your company.

I am available for an interview at your convenience. I may be reached at 201-555-8747 during the day or 201-555-1176 in the evenings.

Thank you for your consideration.

Sincerely,

Gayle McNerney

Self-Referral Letter Based on an Informational Interview

Dear Ms. McCloud:

I'm sure you remember my conducting an informational interview with you last November. The insight you provided into the interior design world was invaluable to me, and I thank you again for giving so generously of your time and information. I'm now starting my job search in earnest and would like to meet with you again to discuss the possibility of joining your firm.

In my most recent position as an architectural assistant, I headed up activities ranging from complete coordination and production of construction drawings to space planning and design development. I met with clients, identified their needs, and executed their space plans in New York and Philadelphia. As my previous employer can attest, my work was accurate and detail oriented.

I've been impressed by the exceptional work McCloud Interiors does, and I'm convinced that I can enhance the firm's success.

Ms. McCloud, I am confident that my qualifications are an excellent fit with the position and that it would be mutually beneficial for us to meet. I will call you early next week to set up an appointment for an interview.

Sincerely,

Marty Panich

Self-Referral Letter Based on Previous Correspondence

Dear Mr. Richards:

Back in January, before I located to Rochester from Great Neck, I wrote to you about the possibility of employment with your organization. You responded with an extremely encouraging letter. You said that with my qualifications, I should have no difficulty finding a job here.

I'm happy to say you were right. I'm working as the legal affairs coordinator in the Department of Public Works. Having gotten such a warm reception from you in your very kind letter, I thought you might like to know that I am here in Rochester and am enhancing my ability to make a contribution to an organization such as yours.

I am well versed in cutting-edge environmental issues. And, having worked as a lobbyist for the Atlantic Coast Preservation League, I am also highly adept in lobbying state, local, and federal governmental entities on important environmental issues.

Mr. Richards, I have enclosed some of my position papers. I am positive that it would be constructive for us to meet. I would like to be considered for a lobbyist position. I'm convinced that my qualifications and your needs are a perfect match.

I'll check in with you at the Environmental Awards luncheon next week. You may also wish to reach me; during business hours, you can call 555-4800 or leave a message on my home machine at 555-2010.

I appreciate your consideration, and thanks again for your wonderful letter in January.

Cordially,

Joshua Abrahms

Self-Referral Letter Based on a Phone Conversation

Dear Ms. Bowman:

I thoroughly enjoyed speaking with you on the phone last week. When you informed me of the upcoming vacancy in your travel services department, I was thrilled. My solid experience in customer service makes me a perfect candidate for the Travel Counselor position.

My background in the corporate travel industry has helped me to become extremely adept at making optimal travel arrangements, providing business services of all kinds, and functioning as a productive team member. I understand the needs of the business traveler who seeks practical, yet comfortable, arrangements.

My strong organizational skills would serve me well in saving clients money and identifying the most efficient and enjoyable means of travel. My former employers will attest that I work extremely well and produce timely results under pressure and that I possess exceptional telephone and customer-service skills.

I am convinced that I would be an asset to your team. I will contact you in ten days to arrange an appointment for us to meet in person. Should you wish to speak to me in the meantime, you may reach me at 414-555-2010.

Once again, it was wonderful to talk with you, and thank you for considering my qualifications.

Sincerely,

Misha Gabriel

CHAPTER 27

THE NEEDS-FULFILLMENT COVER LETTER

One of the most powerful aspects of networking, and especially informational interviewing, is the opportunity to find out about an employer's needs. Every need discovered is an opportunity. During your networking and informational interviewing, be alert to problems you could solve, gaps you could fill, situations you could improve. After all, employers look for those who can fulfill their needs. Networking and informational interviewing give you an opportunity to uncover and tap into an organization's needs—often even before the company has begun to address the need. It's a priceless technique because not only can you describe yourself as the perfect person to meet the need, but you can also make yourself a shining star in the employer's eyes for showing awareness of and concern for the firm's well-being. Following are examples of this approach:

Dear Mr. Zwanger:

I enjoyed chatting with you last week at the Manufacturers Association dinner. I recall our discussion about the difficulties you've been having in meeting your production schedules. I've been giving considerable thought to your dilemma and have come up with some ideas. I wondered if we might be able to get together so I can share my thoughts with you.

As you know, I am the foreman at Supplee and Company. I've developed a highly effective scheduling system; we have not missed a deadline in seven years. I'd really like to bring this scheduling success to Eastwood.

I'll give you a call next week to see if we can arrange a time to continue our conversation.

Sincerely,

Sid Ross

Dear Ms. Stevens:

Your coworker Andrea Kirkwood suggested I contact you about a position in your real estate office. When I interviewed Ms. Kirkwood six months ago to obtain information about a career in real estate, she mentioned that the agency would like to establish a web presence. I'd like to combine my interest in real estate with my knowledge of web page design and HTML programming to help create a webmaster position in your office. I've sketched out some preliminary ideas of what your web page might look like, and I'd love to get together and show them to you.

While I have recently begun training for my real estate license, I've been an art director/graphic artist at PacificWeb for more than two years. I began my Internet-design career by working with numerous local and national companies. With these assignments, I've used my creative problem-solving abilities to create websites that are informative, eye-catching, and easy to use.

I am convinced that you would love my ideas for your website. I will contact you in ten days to arrange a time when we can meet. Should you have any questions before my call, please don't hesitate to contact me at 555-8408. Thanks so much for your consideration.

Cordially,

Cynthia Phillips

RESOURCES

This list of resources is not exhaustive, but it provides a good sampling of networking tools and organizations. The categories of resources, in which items are arranged alphabetically, include

- General networking organizations

- General professional organizations and associations

- Women's networking and professional organizations

- Minority networking and professional organizations

- Companies that produce speed-networking events

- Internet networking tools

- Print and Internet networking/job-search publications

A website address and brief description are provided for each resource. Many resources require a fee or dues. Descriptions of resources have been, for the most part, provided by the organizations themselves. Keep in mind that websites are subject to change; they frequently change addresses or cease to exist. If you come across an outdated web address here, check for updates at the "A Foot in the Door Networking Resources" section of the Quintessential Careers website at www.quintcareers.com/networking.html.

General Networking Organizations

All Cities Resource Group
http://allcities.org
California organization that sponsors a series of networking business groups that meet monthly.

Business Networking International (BNI)
www.bni.com
Offers members the opportunity to share ideas, contacts, and business referrals.

Execunet
www.execunet.com
Network for executive jobs, career, and executive recruiting solutions.

Five O'Clock Club
www.fiveoclockclub.com
Career coaching and outplacement network for professionals, managers, and executives.

Forty Plus
www.fortyplus.org
Nonprofit organization that provides professional job search programs, networking opportunities, and a wide variety of resources to members, who are executives, managers, and professionals.

Toastmasters International
www.toastmasters.org
Enables members to build confidence by speaking to groups and working with others in a supportive environment.

U.S. Junior Chamber of Commerce (Jaycees)
www.usjaycees.org
Provides leadership development, volunteerism, and community service to men and women 21–39 years of age.

General Professional Organizations and Associations

Since thousands of professional organizations are available, the best resources in this area are tools that help you find professional organizations and associations in your field.

Associations on the Net
www.ipl.org/div/aon/
Lists organizations that have a web presence, enabling you to explore groups you might want to join.

Encyclopedia of Associations
www.gale.com/servlet/Browse SeriesServlet?region=9&imprint= 000&cf=ps&titleCode=EA1&dc =null&dewey=null&edition=
Library reference book, published by Gale Research, Incorporated.

Gateway to Associations On-line
www.asaecenter.org/Directories/ AssociationSearch.cfm?navItem Number=16581
Provides a comprehensive directory of websites of business and professional associations.

Women's Networking and Professional Organizations

WOMEN'S NETWORKING ORGANIZATIONS

Advancing Women
www.advancingwomen.com
Highlights issues for the working woman. Includes an online career center, Today's Women's News feature, forums for discussion, links for networking with international women, personal services resources, and links to similar sites.

American Association of University Women
www.aauw.org
A national organization that promotes education and equity for all women and girls.

American Business Women's Association
www.abwa.org
An association dedicated to the promotion of women through leadership, networking support, education, and national recognition.

Business and Professional Women USA
www.bpwusa.org
Hosts meetings to discuss issues such as equity, job advancement, and networking.

National Association for Female Executives (NAFE)
www.nafe.com
Provides resources and services through education, networking, and public advocacy to empower its members to achieve career success and financial security.

National Association of Women Business Owners
www.nawbo.org
Leadership training and a network for women who have been in business for themselves for more than eight years.

National Women's Political Caucus
www.nwpc.org
Leadership and campaign-training programs.

WOMEN'S PROFESSIONAL ORGANIZATIONS

A limited selection of women's professional organizations is provided here.

American Medical Women's Association
www.amwa-doc.org
Serves female health professionals.

American Woman's Society of Certified Public Accountants (AWSCPA)
www.awscpa.org
Devoted exclusively to the support and professional development of women CPAs.

American Women in Radio and Television
www.awrt.org
Serves women working in electronic media and related fields.

Association for Women in Communications
www.womcom.org
Champions the advancement of women across communications disciplines.

Association for Women in Development
www.awid.org
International membership organization connecting, informing, and mobilizing people and organizations committed to achieving gender equality, sustainable development, and women's human rights.

Association for Women in Science (AWIS)
www.awis.org
Dedicated to achieving equity and full participation for women in science, mathematics, engineering, and technology.

Association of Women in International Trade
www.wiit.org
Provides networking and educational opportunities to women involved in international trade and business.

Commercial Real Estate Women
www.nncrew.org
For women working in all facets of commercial real estate.

Federally Employed Women
www.few.org
Works for advancement of women in government.

Financial Women International
www.fwi.org
Exists to help women in the banking and financial services industry learn, lead, and succeed.

International Alliance for Women in Music
www.iawm.org
Serves composers, conductors, performers, and music lovers; provides venues for female artists to perform; and helps promote their shows.

National Association of Insurance Women
www.naiw.org
Provides opportunities for women in the insurance industry to expand their circles of business contacts and knowledge through association activities.

Organization of Women in International Trade (OWIT)
www.owit.org
Promotes women doing business in international trade by providing networking and educational opportunities.

Society of Women Engineers
www.swe.org
Empowers women to succeed and advance in their aspirations and be recognized for their life-changing contributions and achievements as engineers and leaders.

Women in Housing and Finance
www.whfdc.org
Professional and nonpartisan association of women and men in the fields of financial services, housing, and housing finance.

Women in International Security
http://wiis.georgetown.edu
Dedicated to enhancing opportunities for women working in foreign and defense policy.

Women in Technology International
www.witi.com
Provides access to people and content that are relevant to the issues faced by women in technology.

Women's Caucus for the Arts
www.nationalwca.com
Expands opportunities and recognition for women in the arts.

Women's National Book Association
www.wnba-books.org
Serves women in publishing, writing, and editing, as well as those who have an interest in books.

Minority Networking and Professional Organizations

As with women's resources, a limited selection of minority networking/professional organizations and websites is provided here.

African American Business Link
www.aabl.com
A directory and communication center for African American–owned businesses and organizations.

Black Career Women
www.bcw.org
National professional development organization.

Hispanic Online
www.hisp.com
An online forum on the Web for Latinos living in the United States.

LatPro Network
www.latpro.com
Extensive network of career sites in the Hispanic community.

National Association of Asian American Professionals
www.naaap.org
Proving ground for North American Asian professionals, forging leaders of tomorrow through professional development, cultural awareness, and community service.

National Association of Black Accountants, Inc.
www.nabainc.org
Promotes greater participation by minorities in the accounting profession.

National Association of Negro Business and Professional Women's Clubs
www.nanbpwc.org
Encourages youth and young adults to achieve economic independence.

National Black MBA Association
www.nbmbaa.org
Business organization that works to create economic and intellectual wealth for the black community.

The National Black Programmers Coalition
www.nbpcinc.com
An organization of professionals who have united forces to promote positive ideas and education and to generate resources that will enhance the radio and record industry for the betterment of its members.

National Council of Negro Women, Inc.
www.ncnw.org
A nonprofit organization that works at the national, state, local, and international levels in pursuit of the goal to "leave no one behind" and improve quality of life for women, children, and families.

National Organization of Black Law Enforcement Executives
www.noblenatl.org
Offers training in cultural diversity, community policing, and law enforcement issues.

National Society for Hispanic Professionals
www.nshp.org
Society to empower Hispanic professionals with networking and leadership opportunities and to provide information on education, careers, and entrepreneurship.

National Society of Black Engineers
www.nsbe.org
Mission is to increase the number of culturally responsible black engineers who excel academically, succeed professionally, and positively impact the community.

National Society of Hispanic MBAs
www.nshmba.org
Provides career networking opportunities for Hispanic business professionals.

Native Web Community Center
www.nativeweb.org
Brings together indigenous peoples around the world by providing the tools and resources needed to communicate.

Organization of Black Designers
www.obd.org
Community of African American design professionals.

United States Hispanic Chamber of Commerce
www.ushcc.com
Highlights business opportunities for Hispanic entrepreneurs.

Companies That Produce Speed-Networking Events

High Speed Networking
www.networkingforprofessionals.com/HighSpeedNetworking.php
Users can find speed-networking events.

SpeedNetworking.com
www.speednetworking.com
Enables users to organize and host speed-networking events.

Internet Networking Tools
ONLINE DISCUSSION GROUPS

CataList
www.lsoft.com/lists/listref.html
Online catalog of groups that operate using Listserv software.

Delphi Forums
www.delphiforums.com
Network of member-managed online communities.

ezboard
www.ezboard.com
Network of more than 300,000 online communities inhabited by businesses and individuals covering a wide range of topics and interests.

Google Groups
http://groups.google.com
Enables users to search for discussion groups in their career field by entering a keyword.

listTool.com
www.listtool.com
A free tool that simplifies the process of subscribing, unsubscribing, and sending commands to 800+ mailing and discussion lists.

Tribe.net
http://cluster.tribe.net/tribe/servlet/
Enables users to connect with people—family, school friends, coworkers —as well as join and create "Tribes" around interest areas.

Yahoo Groups
http://groups.yahoo.com
Users can join or start a group on just about any topic.

EMPLOYMENT-ISSUES DISCUSSION GROUPS

Ask the Headhunter
http://boards.fool.com/messages.asp?
id=1040001000000000
Discussion on employment topics.

Monster's Career Advice Community
http://monster.prospero.com/n/forum
Index.aspx? webtag=monsterindex
Offers a wide variety of bulletin boards/chats that enable users to network on topics of interest to job seekers.

WetFeet Discussion Boards
www.wetfeet.com/discuss/home.asp
Offers a number of active discussion boards.

WEB-BASED NETWORKING/ONLINE COMMUNITIES

Company of Friends
www.fastcompany.com/cof
Fast Company magazine's global readers' network.

Ecademy.com
http://ecademy.com
Business network that connects people to each other—enabling knowledge, contacts, and opportunities to be shared for worldwide wealth

everyonesconnected.com
http://everyonesconnected.com
Enables users to meet people through friends they already know.

Facebook
http://facebook.com
Social utility that connects people with those around them.

Friendster
www.friendster.com
Online community that connects people through networks of friends for dating, making new friends, and helping friends meet new people.

hi5
www.hi5.com
An online networking site for meeting new people, connecting with friends, and sharing ideas.

JibberJobber
www.jibberjobber.com/networking.php
Enables users to enter, track, log, and manage networking relationships.

Jigsaw
www.jigsaw.com
An online business contact marketplace where marketers, recruiters, and salespeople can buy, sell, and trade business contact information.

LinkedIn
www.LinkedIn.com
Enables users to make deals, as well as find employees, industry experts, jobs, and contracts by making contact with other professionals.

MediaBistro
http://mediabistro.com
Provides online and offline opportunities for meeting each other, sharing resources, becoming informed of job opportunities and interesting projects, improving career skills, and showcasing work.

Meetup
http://meetup.com
Helps people get together with groups of neighbors who share a common interest.

MySpace
www.myspace.com
Online community that lets users meet their friends' friends.

MyWorkster.com
www.myworkster.com
Connects business professionals and college students, where users can build and expand networks of contacts, begin networking for job opportunities and job leads, join groups.

NetParty
www.netparty.com
Provides access to business and social networking events for young professionals.

Networking for Professionals
www.networkingforprofessionals.com
An online networking group designed for professionals from numerous occupations.

PowerMingle.com
www.powermingle.com
Where professionals can meet, mingle, and network with other professionals.

Real Contacts
www.realcontacts.com
Networking site for job seekers that enables sustained contact with one's network.

Ryze
http://ryze.com
Helps people make connections and grow their networks.

The Virtual Handshake
www.on-linebusinessnetworks.com
Resource for learning more about building relationships online— for job hunting or freelancers searching for new clients. Includes detailed reviews of online networking resources, as well as other networking tools.

Xing
www.xing.com
European business network that allows users to establish new business contacts, systematically grow their networks, manage existing contact information, and more.

Yahoo 360
http://360.yahoo.com/l
Enables users to share blogs, photos, lists, recommendations, and more.

ZoomInfo
www.zoominfo.com
Business information search engine.

SCHOOL ALUMNI NETWORKING GROUPS

Alumni.NET
www.alumni.net
Offers links to high schools and colleges located around the U.S. and the world.

Classmates
www.classmates.com
Provides four databases—high schools, colleges, military, and workplace.

Reunion.com
www.reunion.com
Alumni of any American high school can visit this site and register, update information, or search for an old classmate.

EMPLOYER ALUMNI NETWORKING GROUPS

Corporate Alumni Inc.
www.corporatealumni.com
Designs, manages, and hosts communities composed of former employees of companies.

TOOLS FOR FINDING PEOPLE ON THE INTERNET

PeopleSpot
www.peoplespot.com
Portal for numerous search engines that provide email search, reverse searches, special directories, U.S. white pages, international white pages, zip codes.

Ziggs
www.ziggs.com
Offers a search platform for professionals for finding people in business online.

CHAT/ICQ/INSTANT MESSAGING

Numerous chat venues exist on the Internet. The best way to find out everything you need to know about chatting and download the software you need for it is to go to *http://download.com.com/3150-2150-0.html?tag=dir.*

You can also get free downloads of the three most popular instant-messaging applications:

AOL Instant Messenger and ICQ at *http://discover.aol.com/downloads/*

MSN Messenger for PC: *www.microsoft.com/downloads/details.aspx?FamilyID=d78f2ff1-79ea-4066-8ba0-ddbed94864fc&DisplayLang=en*

MSN Messenger for Mac: *www.microsoft.com/mac/default.aspx?pid=msnmessenger*

Talk City
www.talkcity.com
Chat and community site.

Yahoo Messenger at *http://messenger.yahoo.com/webmessengerpromo.php*

VISIBILITY TOOLS/FREE HOSTING FOR WEBSITES

A web page of your own can be a helpful networking tool because it provides a way for prospective contacts to find you and can include a portfolio, a blog, and other items.

FreeWebspace.Net
www.freewebspace.net
Search engine that enables you to find websites with free web space hosting.

Squidoo
http://squidoo.com
Enables users to become "lensmasters" and demonstrate their expertise in a field by creating a Squidoo web page.

BLOGGING RESOURCES

A blog is another way to boost your networking visibility.

Blogger
www.blogger.com
Site for creating free blogs.

Greymatter
www.noahgrey.com/greysoft/
Open source blogging and journal software.

Live Journal
www.livejournal.com
Tools for private journaling, blogging, holding a discussion forum, social networking.

Xanga
www.xanga.com
Blogging platform.

Print and Internet Networking/Job-Search Publications

Bolles, Richard Nelson. *What Color Is Your Parachute?: A Practical Manual for Job-Hunters and Career-Changers*. Berkeley, California: Ten Speed Press, updated annually. www.tenspeed.com. The classic job-search guide.

Fraser, George, and Les Brown. *Success Runs in Our Race: The Complete Guide to Effective Networking in the Black Community*. Rev. ed. New York: Amistad, 2004. www.harpercollins .com. (See also George Fraser's website: www.frasernet.com.) Excellent guide for networkers of all ethnicities.

Hansen, Katharine. *Dynamic Cover Letters for New Graduates*. Berkeley, California: Ten Speed Press, 1998. www.tenspeed.com. Cover letters especially for college students and new grads.

Hansen, Katharine, and Randall Hansen. *Dynamic Cover Letters: How to Sell Yourself to an Employer by Writing a Letter That Will Get Your Resume Read, Get You an Interview, and Get You the Job*. Berkeley, California: Ten Speed Press, 2001. www.tenspeed.com. Comprehensive information about the cover-letter techniques touched on in this book.

Hello, my name is Scott: www .hellomynameisScott.com. Huge collection of networking books, tips, and articles.

Krueger, Brian D. *The College Grad Job Hunter: Insider Techniques and Tactics for Finding a Top-Paying Job*. 6th ed. Holbrook, Massachusetts: Adams Media Corporation, 2008. www.adamsmedia.com. Contains abundant networking tips for college students.

Whitcomb, Susan Britton. *Resume Magic: Trade Secrets of a Professional Resume Writer*. 2nd ed. Indianapolis: Jist Works, 2006. www.jist.com. Comprehensive guide to resume writing.

INDEX